Contents

Leszek Kolakowski

TOWARD A MARXIST HUMANISM

Essays on the Left Today

Translated from the Polish
by Jane Zielonko Peel

Grove Press, Inc.
New York

Toward a Marxist Humanism

Toward a Marxist Humanism

The Priest and the Jester

Twentieth-century thinkers have done everything to keep alive in our minds the main questions that have troubled theologians over the years, though we phrase the questions somewhat differently. Philosophy has never freed itself from its theological heritage, which means that theological questions were merely clumsy formulations of essential enigmas that still hold us in thrall.

Enigmas? Perhaps it is not always a matter of what is really enigmatic, but very often of a situation that we read a riddle into because the most obvious and irrefutable facts seem unacceptable to us.

Indeed, nothing is as deeply rooted in us as the belief in a moral law that is the ultimate moderator, the conviction that the world we live in will eventually reach a state in which our merits and rewards, our crimes and punishments will be evened out, where evil will be avenged and good find its recompense, and every account of wrongs will be settled—in other words, where human values will be fully realized. Whatever happens, we can rejoice, for abundant rewards await us in heaven.

Thus the first question contemporary philosophy has taken over from the theological tradition is that of the very possibility of eschatology itself. We put it otherwise, to all appearances nontheologically: Can the human values we accept attain complete realization? Does history evolve in a defined direction that promises ultimate equalization and universal justice? No wonder we ask ourselves such questions. Reflection on history has its main source in our discontent with its results; the most common hope of historiosophy is to identify or adjust the essence of man with his existence; that is, to assure that the unalterable aspirations of human nature will be fulfilled in reality. Since this would put an end to the dissatisfaction with history's results that gives birth to historiosophy, we can say that the latter has chosen as its chief

9

hope a situation that leads to its own extinction. In any case, every optimistic historiosophy is incurably suicidal.

This secular eschatology, this belief in the future elimination of the disparity between man's essence and his existence (in the deification of man), presupposes, obviously, that "essence" is a value, that its realization is desirable, and that the wisdom of history will bring about this realization. Secular eschatology trusts in the final judgment of history. We do not laugh at this belief, for who is not susceptible to it? For example, whenever someone expects the misfortunes and suffering of the dead to be avenged by history, or "age-old accounts of wrongs" to be settled, he demonstrates his belief in the last judgment. Whenever he assumes that "human nature's" desires will some day be satisfied, he reveals his faith in eschatology, in the end of the world, and thus in man's finiteness. Accepting the validity of an eschatology is one of the principal problems of contemporary historiosophy, and therefore of a contemporary outlook on the world. Ever since the eighteenth century in Europe, from the first moment when "History" and "Progress" stole onto the throne of Jehovah, who had been deposed by violence, it has been evident that they could successfully replace him in his chief functions. Once historical eschatology had demonstrated its possibilities, human history became a cogent argument for atheism, for it had become known that another force could take the burden of God upon itself and lull the unfortunate with a vision of a happy ending in which their torment and efforts would be rewarded.

Not every conviction that historical "progress" occurs need be eschatological, after all. Belief in progress, in the applicability of evaluative criteria to historical facts, does not compel us to have chiliastic visions. The latter require the additional assumption that current history can be characterized by its striving toward a lasting goal that can be defined and that will irrevocably end all existing conflicts. It is irrelevant whether one calls this result the end of history or its beginning: for every eschatology, the end of earthly history is the end of a history of trial and tribulation and simultaneously the beginning of the life of the blessed, of which we know nothing except that it will be a state of eternal rapture and content.

The question whether eschatology is possible—regardless of whether the answer is negative or positive—is one of the central problems of what we may call philosophical anthropology, which today includes most of the vital issues of philosophy. But theology has never been more than a projection of anthropology onto non-human reality. To resolve the antagonisms of "human nature"—those between the natural aspirations of man's essence and his involvement in his external fate—contemporary philosophical anthropology may still search for solutions either in transcendency as the Christian existentialists (Jaspers, Marcel) do, or in history as do the Marxists, or else it may declare the conflict irresolvable. The latter position was once formulated by Freud; today the atheistic existentialists state it differently. But regardless of the arguments expressed in more or less "technical" language, the question itself is common currency, and almost everyone, under the combined or conflicting pressures of tradition and personal experience, has a ready answer to it. In this popular version the replies need not be theses; most are attitudes toward life that express, though perhaps subconsciously, a solution to this problem: Is the life of each of us simply a collection of consecutive facts in the process of occurring, each one consumed in the time of its duration, or is each fact something more than the content of its time span—an expectation, a hope for other facts not yet completed, the revelation of a certain fragment of the final prospect of fulfillment? Is every fact a self-contained reality, or is it a section of a road at whose end consolation and peace await us? The reply to this question has a highly practical value, for it determines how we are going to regard our daily endeavors. Will we consider them a kind of scraping together of pennies toward a pension fund for ourselves or for mankind, and thus run the risk of scorning current facts and momentary values? Or will we, on the contrary, see in them only their empirical and immediate content, and so squander possibilities that can be realized only after certain preparations and that require a transcendental interpretation of facts, one that imparts sense to a fact by relating it to something beyond? To risk losing current values in exchange for ultimate, though perhaps illusory, ones, or on the other hand, to risk losing greater values by wasting one's life on current ones—what could be more banal than these two poles between which our daily life oscillates? Yet this is precisely what philosophy speaks about, having inherited the problem from theology. We can readily see how the force that attracts these two poles is dominated by one or the other of the two factors that make us try to resolve this problem: the need for consolation after the suffering of everyday life, opposed to the fear of submerging one's life in fictions, a fear that grows proportionately with the disillusionments of experience.

The next question, directly connected to the preceding one, is that of theodicy, and it too belongs to the theological legacy of modern thought. In its modernized version it concerns the rationalism of history, the question whether the individual's misfortunes and suffering have meaning and justification within a universal historical rationality. Traditional theodicy teaches us that God's infallible justice shines in the misery of the condemned, and that in human unhappiness the glory of the highest good becomes manifest. There is a difference between the problem formulated above and the one posed by theodicy. Eschatology tries to give meaning to all facts by relating them to an ultimate completion; theodicy tries to justify partial evil by linking it to the order of a wisely conceived whole, omitting the question of whether such justification is to be found in the ultimate completion.

The problem of theodicy in its modern version is that of the "wisdom" of history—of devising such an intellectual organization of the world that the evil we know or experience reveals its "sense" and value interwoven in the wise plans of history. Ideologies based on theodicy need not necessarily be conservative, although most historical examples rather incline us toward the generalization that they are. Strictly speaking, theodicy is conservative whenever it justifies evil that people experience independently of their decisions; it is not necessarily so if it merely justifies evil brought on by one's own free choice. In the first instance, it is simply the ideology of man's helplessness in the face of the conditions of his life, a mystification that compensates for and lends value to our resignation from all effort to change the world. In the second, it can be an ideology that sanctions our risks in participating in human conflicts, whether on the side of good or of evil.

Theodicy belongs to the field of popular philosophy, the philosophy of everyday life. Although it sometimes takes the form of historiosophical abstractions, its acceptance or rejection is expressed in common attitudes, in that semiconscious practical philosophy which influences human behavior. On this level its action varies. A person who has suffered an irreparable misfortune can find consolation in the thought that God's unerring finger has designated his misery to create in this world some good unknown to him; or else in the thought that nothing in human history happens without a reason, nothing is wasted, and every torment of the individual is scrupulously entered in the ledgers of the bank of history and enriches the account from which future generations will draw interest. Those who can take such convictions to heart can certainly derive great benefits from them, and there would be no reason to rob them of this source of comfort if they did not apply it as well to reversible misfortunes or to evils which can be opposed. But most often theodicies do serve in just such situations. The conviction that by the will of God or of history nothing in human life is in vain is so powerful an encouragement to our innate inertia and such a sanctification of our conservatism and laziness that in practical life it shields inertia against pangs of conscience and rational criticism.

"Ultimately," it is easy to say to oneself, "our fate is only a small part of the universe, a fragment of that enormous whole wherein the suffering of the individual serves to increase the general good, where everything influences everything else while a certain enduring order is maintained. Whatever evil occurs is a sacrifice on the altar of the whole; and sacrifices are not made in vain." Though sober observation does not vindicate this optimism —though it seems instead to indicate that there is no historical scale on which an individual's fate is balanced; that some human torment certainly does benefit others, while other suffering serves no purpose and is simply what it is, bare suffering; that many troubles and sacrifices as well as many lives are ultimately in vain and there is no proof that they amount to anything else—though this integrating and compensatory vision of the world finds no support in our knowledge of reality, it is so strongly rooted in our longings for recompense that it appears to be one of the most obstinate intellectual prejudices of all time. Let me say again that criticism would not be to the point if this prejudice functioned merely as a soothing interpretation of past and irrevocable events and not also as an apology for existing stituations whose inevitability is far from proved.

Theodicy is, therefore, a method of transforming facts into values; that is, a method through which a fact becomes not what it appears to be empirically, but an element in a teleological order that bestows special significance on all its components. To perceive values in facts is without doubt a legacy from magical thinking, older than speculative philosophies, which assumes a belief in the sanctifying or damning power of certain events, unrelated to their empirical characteristics but derived from their invisible attributes. The conviction that our current and real suffering must have its counterpart in future good presupposes a belief in certain invisible, secret qualities of unpleasant events, qualities that are bound to the wise order of the universe and take on value from it. This conviction is of the same type as any belief in magic. The point here is not to criticize such concepts, but to bring out the essential points in which thinking, modern secular philosophical thinking included, is forced to reply either negatively or positively to questions out of not merely a theological, but also a pretheological, magical tradition. Every belief or disbelief that a God-less history or a God-less universe organizes its elements into a teleological unity and imparts value to them as properties independent of our ideas is a belief or disbelief in theodicy. I do not mean to say that the question itself is superficial. The question of the existence of an order immanent in the world is not merely apparent, and we tacitly confirm this whenever we agree to answer it, however negatively. We thus testify to the meaningfulness of theodicy, for presupposing that a question is worthy of an answer, we assume a certain reason for the existence of the field of knowledge in which the question originates. Theodicy is therefore a part of contemporary philosophy, whether it is called the metaphysics of values, or a consideration of man's place in the cosmos, or a discussion of historical progress. All three cases, which are among the staples of contemporary nonreligious philosophy, show that the patronage of theodicy, and through it of magic, has not become obsolete.

The belief in eschatology, like the belief in theodicy, is an attempt to find absolute justification for our life outside its limits, to establish a reality that makes all other reality meaningful and comprehensible, and that itself requires no further interpretation by reference to something else. The absolute usually becomes a moral support because it is metaphysical, because in a metaphysical construction of the world individuals appear as manifestations or instances and become understandable only as such. But the role of the absolute emerges more directly in other questions whose pertinence to the history of theology is known, and which in modern form still trouble not only philosophers but all who seek some reason for their own behavior.

The most important of these questions is the problem of nature and grace. Throughout the principal conflicts that mark the history of Christianity it was one of the central problems (Pelagianism, the Reformation, Jansenism), together with that of theodicy (the Manichaeans, the Cathari) and of redemption (Monophysites, Arians, Socinians). It is easy to see that this question of the relation between individual responsibility and external determinants is no less alive today than it was at the time of the Council of Trent, and no less complicated and difficult. In its most general form the question concerns determinism and responsibility: in what sense and to what degree the individual "can" or "cannot" resist the influence of independent forces that shape his behavior, and in what sense he is, in view of this, morally responsible for himself and to what degree he can place this responsibility on those forces over which he has no control. There are many variations on this problem—biological, sociological, historiosophical, metaphysical—yet the sources of social interest in it remain the same as in the past. Some variations now have a chance of being studied and resolved empirically, thus losing their philosophical character. Others have remained within the boundaries of historiosophical or metaphysical speculation, without much prospect of another kind of solution. In all of them, however, we try to find out how certain factors independent of us—either physiological or historical—can ex post facto justify us, or else to what degree they can supply us with infallible guidelines for future decisions. Above all, there has grown up around historical determinism an intricate complex of questions that attract attention as among the most vital in contemporary philosophical thinking.

"We do not have the freedom to do this or that, but only the freedom to do what is necessary or else nothing at all. And the task that historical necessity has set is carried out with the individual or against him." This attitude concisely summarizes the idea of historical predestination, against which any revolt is foredoomed to fail. At the same time the idea justifies acts undertaken in accordance with the innate inevitability of history. The words quoted are the ending of Spengler's *The Decline of the West*, but they can serve as an emphatic formula for a more universal tendency. All concepts of natural cycles of civilization —like Arnold Toynbee's—are analogous to the world vision of *De Civitate Dei*. Opponents of historical determinism—Isaiah Berlin, Karl Popper—continue, in this sense, the Pelagian idea of salvation. Marxist literature on the subject presents various motifs, usually revolving around solutions close to those of the Council of Trent: Actions that correspond to the desires of the historical absolute move within the framework of determination derived from that absolute. Nevertheless, there is no irresistible grace, and the individual bears responsibility for accepting or rejecting the offer of cooperation that the absolute extends to everyone. Redemption is available to everyone, yet on the other hand not all will take advantage of it, and therefore the human race is inevitably divided into the chosen and the rejected. This division is irrevocably planned by the absolute and all its consequences are preordained; nonetheless, individuals freely enter one or the other category.

This analogy is not meant to ridicule a topic that is alive today in philosophy, but to disclose the latent rationality of these theological issues that have lost their vitality in their previous form. For it is not surprising that the basic difficulties inherent in any world view have a stubbornly persistent character, whereas our degree of culture and the resources of our vocabulary define how we express them. Our explanations are therefore directed at most against enlightened and free-thinking persons' disdain of questions that preoccupied past ages—as if we ourselves were not trying to solve the selfsame problems using a different technique. This scorn is as unreasonable as it would be to laugh at medieval man for using horses instead of jet planes to move from place to place, if horses were the most rational transportation method he had. Today airplanes serve the same purpose more efficiently, just as historiosophical thinking deals more effectively with the same difficulties that disputes about the Trinity and irresistible grace once tried to solve. It is not surprising that we long to understand what part forces independent of us play in our behavior. Nor need we wonder that in this search we would often like to penetrate not only those forces which act upon us as energy transmitters, but also elementary and autonomous forces —the absolute. If this absolute is the historical process, secular historiosophy simply assumes the tasks of theology, which had obviously become an anachronism in its old version.

Deliberation upon nature and grace can serve a manifold purpose: it may seek a principle in whose decisions we can have total confidence and which takes our responsibility upon itself, dispelling all conflicts; it may be concerned with a highest tribunal on whose mercy we can throw ourselves fearlessly, certain it will allow no harm to befall us if we follow its instructions, and will reward our obedience liberally; or it may simply be a quest for assurance that in this life we have chosen the better side and that consequently everything we do in its name is just. Some answers to the problem of nature and grace serve to annul our responsibility, which the absolute assumes entirely: this is the Calvinist solution. Others accept responsibility, but on condition that our acts be governed by clearly formulated rules whose observance insures effective results: this is the Catholic solution. Still others accept the principle of unconditional responsibility toward the absolute, but with the risk of uncertainty about the intentions of the lawgiver: this is the Jansenist solution. In every instance it is assumed that the absolute incorporates within itself both legislative and judicial powers; a subtle dispute is waged as to the area in which it is also the executive. Another argument tries to ascertain whether the absolute's decrees can be clearly known to man and, if so, precisely how; whether, if they are known, they can be executed; and whether, if they are not adequately known, the transgressor can excuse himself on grounds of ignorance of the law. It was on such questions that sixteenth- and seventeenth-century theological debates focused—questions of nature and grace, of predestination, and of justification through faith or works. The very existence of a principle that is both the source of all obligation and the tribunal that judges whether the duty was performed in each case was not a subject of controversy at that time. Those who today totally reject the existence of such a principle are simply replying negatively to a question whose answer theology prejudged to be so obviously affirmative that it was not always even formulated.

If we subtract the social conflicts that influence the dispute over nature and grace, we can readily observe two opposing tendencies in regard to individual motivation. On the one hand there is the desire to find support for one's own existence outside oneself, with a corollary fear of individual, isolated existence dependent on one's own decisions, and thus ultimately a longing to discard one's self, to jump out of one's skin. On the other hand lies the fear of the unreality of one's behavior and decisions, of a certain alien force inside us which is not only the executor of our intentions but also the will that initiates them in our stead. The conflict between the pursuit of individual self-affirmation and the drive toward self-destruction—in other words, between the fear of discarding one's self and the fear of one's self—can be termed the universal content of philosophical thinking; more precisely, the history of philosophy proves that this conflict actually does exist.

Let us note, incidentally, that the problem of original sin, which is closely bound to that of nature and grace, has also taken on a modified contemporary form; it deals with the satanic element in man, and thus with the revolt against absolute power. In its modern version it concerns utopia, that is, the attempt to conquer the historical absolute, a power against which all rebellion seems foredoomed. The problem of redemption and incarnation also has a certain secular interpretation: the question of the individual's role in history; that is, of the mechanism by which the historical absolute becomes incorporated in certain exceptional persons, or, more generally, whether these persons draw their energy from transcendent sources or whether they constitute a spontaneous "creative principle" in history.

All these questions involve the relationship between man and the absolute, a subject historiosophy has inherited from theology. However, there are also many questions outside the realm of historiosophy and essential to epistemology which spring from the same source.

Of this group the one which has retained the most validity is revelation. A capricious deity never completely reveals its secrets; nonetheless, a dim reflection of its wisdom is sometimes accessible to mortals, if their eyes are strong enough to gaze upon it with impunity. Revelation is simply the absolute in the order of cognition, a collection of positive and unquestionable data, our means of communicating with the absolute. We need revelation not in order to know with certainty what the world really is, but to evaluate all the opinions of the world that we encounter. Revelation is therefore destined to be the textbook of the inquisitor. It is a granite throne from which we can pass judgment without risk of error, and without which our rickety skeletons cannot support us. Buttressed by revelation, we can do more than merely move the earth: we can stop it in its tracks.

Revelation is the constant hope of philosophy. And indeed we see that the so-called philosophical "systems" which are supposed to give us certainty as the end result of their search, always give it at the very beginning: on the strength of an almost instinctively accepted order, they begin by establishing certain knowledge, an absolute starting point of all thinking. It would seem that once the beginning is given as absolute, then the end is given as well; that once we have set foot on solid ground, moving upon it is uninteresting. For once we have settled what is sure and unshakable, our subsequent thought runs as smoothly as a glass ball over ice. Revelation is the "first push" to thought, after which the latter rolls on automatically; yet this movement is only apparent, for automatism is the exact antithesis of thinking. Thought, in the narrow sense that concerns us here—that is, creative thought—is precisely the activity which cannot be duplicated by an automaton. Philosophy is the eternal effort to question all that is obvious, and thus the continual disavowal of existing revelations. Nevertheless, the temptation to have a revelation of one's own persistently sets traps for critics. Every philosophy that aspires to become a "system" questions others' revelations only to establish its own; and, really, there are not many methods of thinking which do not tacitly espouse the Thomist principle that the goal of every movement is rest. ("*Impossible est igitur quod natura intendat motum propter seipsum. Intendit igitur quietum per motum. . . .*")

Inherent in this assumption is the conviction that the essence of movement is its opposite, immobility; that motion realizes itself by self-annihilation. In other words, all movement is a deformity, an insufficiency of that which moves. It reveals a need, and need is the negative element of nature; therefore the nature of everything fulfills itself by becoming quiescent. In philosophical thinking this principle manifests itself in the conviction that thought moves only because it is imperfect and only in order to attain an ultimate foothold, perfection, immobility. Thought, like all motion, achieves satisfaction and fulfills its aspirations only when it ceases to be motion, thus when it ceases to be. But the urgent need for finality, for revelation, is one of the easiest needs in the world to satisfy; that is why those who seek it find it almost as soon as they become conscious of their need. And when the revelation is found, when thought achieves its desired satisfaction, philosophy begins to build what it thinks is a "system." Actually, the supposed beginning is the end; the building already has a roof at the moment when it seems to us that we have just laid the cornerstone. Any philosophic finality whatsoever is a substitute for revelation, which allegedly constitutes the starting point for theologians but is, in fact, all that is necessary. For theology begins with the belief that truth has already been given to us, and its intellectual effort consists not of attrition against reality but of assimilation of something which is ready in its entirety.

The basic and historically elementary formula of secular revelation was the Cartesian *cogito*: the attempt to question all that was traditionally obvious and final in such a way that the very act of criticism and destruction was completed only when a new finality, the self-knowledge of one's own thinking process, was achieved. Descartes undertook to criticize with the awareness that criticism must have a limit, and that one rejects the moving sands in order to stand on firm ground. Criticism would have been meaningless to him if it had not stopped at a certain fixed point. Thus the task of criticism was to reach an a-critical point, one not subject to criticism; the aim of criticism was self-annihilation, as the goal of motion was nonmotion, immobility. The detection of the weaknesses of successive revelations was to lead to the discovery of a revelation free from flaws.

The development of post-Cartesian philosophy was to a large degree a spate of imitations of the same procedure; philosophers accepted Descartes' question completely, and with it half his answer, and stubborn attempts to modify the *cogito* formula dragged on into this century. In particular the whole evolution of European idealism has disclosed the characteristic of Cartesian revelation that it shares with all revelations: its point of departure is also its point of arrival. Once the consciousness of the thought process is the ultimate datum of cognition, all of reality becomes incapable of going outside the thought process. In Gilson's words, "When we begin in an immanent world, we also finish in an immanent world." This seems completely natural: reality will always assume in our minds the same nature as the ultimate data from which we try to reconstruct it. To announce that certain data have the privilege of being final is to deny reality to everything that cannot in some manner be reduced to them. Therefore, if the immanent world is the absolute of cognition, then it is, as well, everything cognition can achieve; like Spinoza's *causo sui*, being the starting point of the thinking process it is inevitably its point of arrival, the only world whose reality is defensible. Similarly, those for whom the physical objects of everyday reality constitute the only collection of absolute data must admit that they comprise all possible data. And those who ascribe this property to sensory material will construct the world exclusively out of sensory material. In the movement of philosophical thought, the absolute point of departure predetermines all the rest, and he who stands on the absolute, simply stands still. Any further motion on his part is illusory, like the course of a squirrel in a revolving drum.

And yet the nostalgia for revelation lives on in the heart of philosophy, and the need for ultimate satisfaction never abandons it in any era. Taine's positivism had to find satisfaction in the "ultimate law" or the "eternal axiom" of reality, which discloses the unity of the universe and to which all our knowledge can in some way be reduced. The chief ambition of phenomenology was to present a given reality in an absolute and final sense; and since the reality thus given could not be other than immanent, the idealism of Husserl's later works appears to be the result of the above-mentioned innate logic of a doctrine one of whose main tasks originally was to overcome subjectivism. In Husserl's case, the internal antinomy of this quest for revelation was an illustration of all analogous undertakings. The statement that ultimate data can have only an immanent character whereas transcendent reality comes equipped, as Husserl said, "with a zero-indicator of theoretical cognition," presupposes that ultimate data cannot be constituted without an understandable concept of transcendency, about which one prefers to suspend judgment. However, the very concept of transcendency could not stem from anything but that natural and precritical cognitive attitude whose results were not supposed to be taken into account programmatically. Nevertheless, from time to time it appeared that the very verbalization of the original principle, which attributed an ultimate character to pure phenomena, required a prior use of a concept drawn from outside the realm of pure phenomena. This meant availing oneself of certain data from natural knowledge without which nothing could be brought to fruition. The epistemological absolute seemed to be as weighted down with the ballast of nonabsolute knowledge as the Cartesian *cogito*—the assumption of a fictitious thinker, nothing more than a distilled intellectual substance completely independent of all the content which experience and consequent knowledge have bequeathed it. For the absolute, which we cannot describe without simultaneously describing its opposite, thus betrays its fictitiousness. Criticism presupposes the object of criticism; and our very act of thinking, in which we "put in brackets" transcendent reality, assumes that the latter is a datum of our thinking, no matter how many *distinguo* can be added to the word "datum."

Modern positivism, at least in its initial phase, has not been able to resist the pursuit of the cognitive absolute. In stating that finality is the proper word for the nature of observational judgments, Moritz Schlick simply presented another version of the same operation which, in so many different doctrines, was to provide us with secular substitutes for revelation.

The problem of revelation is that of the existence of ultimate data. It is accompanied by a second question: How far is conceptual thinking capable of expressing and understanding ultimate data? This is the problem of mystery, which in contemporary philosophy belongs, like the preceding questions, to the legacy of theology. In its modern form it concerns the boundaries of rationalism, and thus all questions about the rationality of certain elementary factors of perception and of certain indivisible fragments of reality itself. All the deliberations of personalistic doctrines about the noncommunicable nature of personality are a carry-over into the human sphere of the same questions theology posed to God. Personalism in the metaphysical sense—the monadology of the human world—did not attack theology but appropriated its troubles. And here, as in previous cases, we do not wish to maintain that these troubles were imaginary; the question of the rationality of indivisible entities, such as the human personality, is real. If at one time it was a question about the mystery of the person of God, still it was phrased in sufficiently general terms so that priority of use belongs to the theologians. In the evolution of the very word "persona"—mask— a difficulty was revealed that philosophers have stumbled over ever since. This difficulty is usually resolved by a single easy slogan, "Personality is inexpressible." Even if true, this slogan is as sterile as the statement that God is a mystery to mortal minds.

The problem of the relationship between faith and reason has also taken on a modern form. We meet it whenever we try to find out how much experience and rational thinking can help solve conflicting cognitive situations and what role unprovable factors play in our image of the world. Disputes about the unprovable assumptions of the empirical sciences and about the existence of preferential criteria for contradictory sets of experience have inherited much from the theological tradition. If certain facts cannot be reconciled with a previously accepted body of coherent general assumptions that explain our past experience, to what degree may we ignore these facts or interpret them so they harmonize, though sometimes factitiously, with the system? These are the daily troubles of scientific thinking, akin to the ones that arose when revelation constituted the skeleton around which all our knowledge was organized in a compact "system." At the bottom of these disputes we observe the antagonism of the same two tendencies that expressed themselves in nearly all our earlier questions. On the one hand are the integrationist and monistic tendencies whose hope is, strictly speaking, to embrace the universe in a single formula, or at least to discover a single main principle to explain all reality. On the other is the pluralistic bent, not overworried about coherent knowledge, not ambitious to construct a forest out of single trees, but instead ready to accept each particular fact as an absolute even though, on confrontation, some facts contradict others. It was William James who, in radical formulas, took the antimonistic position in regard to knowledge. If the facts are mutually contradictory, we may accept each of them separately —without getting panicky because we cannot find a general principle or law to encompass them all without friction—for we have no reason to suppose that some inflexible elementary law governs every cranny of the universe and every one of its occurrences. We may admit that the way things happen varies, and that the attempt to collect this variety into a unity is usually gratuitous and artificial. Let every fact be its own explanation and let general knowledge become an elastic reaction to each separate situation. If in a series of experiences the world crumbles before our eyes like a heterogeneous agglomeration of haphazardly accumulated pieces, all we can conclude is that the world is precisely what it seems—chaotic, inconsistent, full of accidents, more like a rubbish heap than a library where every item has its defined place in a catalogued and inventoried whole.

Yet this obsession with monism, this stubborn desire to arrange the world according to some uniform principle, this search for a single magic spell to make reality transparent and decipherable, this pursuit of the philosopher's stone, proves to be more lasting than any other vicissitude of our intellectual development. Philosophy favors this monarchistic predilection all the more readily since each era of great scientific syntheses appears to reveal a more orderly world, constantly offering new general principles that make the older ones seem trivial. It follows that philosophy, especially since it has aspired to become a scientific discipline, has eagerly called upon science to witness its claims. But when it tries to abandon its monistic hopes, it produces the opposite effect: It denounces science and discloses that a scientific organization of our image of the world does not represent an organization actually inherent in the world itself, but one that results from just that propensity in the very nature of the human mind.

The examples used here are attempts to justify theology not by reconstructing it systematically but only by providing individual illustrations. All of them draw their subject matter from speculative scholastic theology, but the wealth of mystic theology has not been lost either; in fact it has retained all its splendor in contemporary thinking.

The problems of mystic theology have remained current particularly in four areas of modern philosophy: the practical interpretation of knowledge; dialectics; an integrating explanation of the world; and questions about the substantiality of original reality.

In the first area, we should note that mystics were the pioneers of a pragmatic approach to cognition. Since the properties of the absolute elude the tools available to human speech, adapted as it is to describing finite things, our only concept of the absolute is practical. Our knowledge, in the strict sense of the word, does not tell us what God is like but advises us how best to worship Him and how, through self-renunciation, to draw nearer to His sublimity. What is more, this knowledge is not so much a collection of recipes one can learn by heart before applying them in practice, as it is their actual application. Reason does not precede will; rather, acts of will become simultaneously acts of reason. We know as much about God as the love we give Him.

Raised by the first pragmatists and still pertinent today, the question of the practical interpretation of knowledge is a generalization of the mystics' program. Let us discard the question of what the world looks like "in and of itself" and treat scientific theories as practical guidelines for our behavior in certain circumstances. Pragmatism is the opposite of realistic epistemology, just as mystic theology was the opposite of speculative theology. Pragmatism rejects as unproductive questions about the nature of reality, replacing them with practical queries.

The second guardian of the treasure bequeathed by mystic theology is dialectics. We know that all attempts to apply current concepts to the absolute have led to contradiction, to antinomy. That is why the mystics became champions of thought that moves from thesis to antithesis. To say that no category of human speech applies to God is to say that whenever we speak of Him we apply all categories to Him. Thus God is and simultaneously is not; He is everything and nothing, the maximum and the minimum, the affirmation and the negation. But we also find the idea of alienation and how to overcome it, the concept of the development of the world as a negation that leads to its opposite, wholly prefigured in mystic texts. The world as the emanation of God, alienated from and, in its finiteness, a negation of its source; and at the same time, in its reverse motion, tending to destroy itself and identify itself once again with its genesis—this vision of Erigena contains almost the whole skeleton of dialectical logic. As in Hegel's logic, alienation need not, however, be a negative phenomenon: the absolute manifests itself through the inevitability of its own nature, and in so doing it somehow enriches itself by manifestations to itself. Similarly, we can consider original sin and man's fall as a necessary stage of development toward his future happiness, upon which he can rely thanks to the Redeemer. *"O felix culpa quae talem ac tantum meruit habere redemptorem,"* says a well-known medieval song. "O blessed sin that merited such a Savior."

Historiosophical deliberations about progress fulfilling itself through its "reverse side," or about alienation to which the human being is subjected so that he can enrich himself by overcoming it, are repetitions of the same theme.

In the third place among mystic theology's contributions to contemporary thought, we have mentioned questions related to the integrating interpretation of existence. The "Gestalt" theory is contained in mystic texts in almost perfect form, though in a very generalized version whose modern equivalent lies in Bergson's speculation rather than in the methodology of the "Gestaltists." Only the absolute possesses a truly independent existence; all the finite fragments we discern in the world, and all the differences among individual things, are either a sort of pathological exclusion that will be abolished when the world returns to the womb of the absolute, or else a distorted picture produced by our imagination, which tries to impose on the indivisible whole its alien principle of multiplicity and differentiation.

The mystics' problem of applying the concept of substance to the absolute has also blossomed anew in our century. The question of whether the original reality has the characteristic of substance, or if substantiality is a secondary phenomenon given to our cognition or even formed by it, while the original reality is something that is not substantial—an event, a relationship, an act—is undoubtedly a question of theological origin. The questioning of the idea of substance in favor of the metaphysical priority of other principles which were traditionally regarded as dependent and predicated upon substance has been expressed in our century in theories that are otherwise entirely different. Giovanni Gentile's actualism, Alfred Whitehead's and Bertrand Russell's theory of events, and Natorp's theory of relations—to mention but three cases of totally dissimilar provenance—meet at a distant genealogical point that would seem quite alien to each of these philosophers. Still, each of us has spiritual ancestors whose portraits we would not care to hang in the family dining room, and of whom the neighbors' malicious gossip reminds us. Besides, I do not deny that these observations bear some resemblance to the famous *Liber Chamorum*, but with the difference that the author does not intend to exclude himself from the infamous register.

So far our list has been merely a loose collection of examples with one aim in common, to demonstrate that many vital problems weighed nowadays by the most divergent philosophical doctrines—as well as by that "everyday" philosophy which always revolves around the same questions as "technical" philosophy— are an extension of theological controversies, or rather a new version of the same tasks whose original and more inept forms we know from the history of theology. And yet, led by the same instinct that, as we have said, is at the root of the monistic predilections of the human spirit and gives birth to monistic interpretations of reality, we also wish to formulate an order-giving principle that will enable us to embrace these conflicting views of the world systematically.

The majority of the examples have revealed an antagonism within philosophy focused on a single theme: for or against eschatology— and thus for or against an ordering of the facts of everyday life in reference to the absolute which is to be realized in the process of development; for or against theodicy—and thus for or against a quest in the absolute for reasons which justify every individual evil in the world; for an interpretation of man in categories of grace, or rather in categories of nature—and thus for or against ascribing responsibility for our acts to the absolute;

for or against revelation—and thus for or against an immutable principle of cognition that is inaccessible to criticism and that constitutes an infallible prop for our thinking; for or against the monistic concept of cognition—and thus for or against intellectual dominion over reality with the help of a set of laws, both the highest and most elementary, which explain everything; for or against a unifying interpretation of the world—and thus for or against a vision that imparts meaning to everything by referring it to the absolute, of which it constitutes a manifestation, a part or instance. In short: for or against the hope of finality in existence and knowledge, for or against a search for support in absolutes.

We have tried to formulate the nature of this conflict as a clash between two universal and primal tendencies to which philosophy seeks to give a discursive form; a situation in which the individual is thrown entirely upon his own resources, a situation of the "indefinability" of the human being, his absolute irreducibility to anything else. This situation instills a fear that is expressed in his search for support in absolute reality, and thus in annihilating himself as an individual, and in his finding a definition for himself and his behavior by referring to something he is not. On the other hand, there is the affirmation of individual existence as an irreducible fact, and thus a rejection of all the reasons that justify individual existence, a denial of any absolute reality, a denial that immobility is the true nature of mobility, a rejection of the prospect of finality.

And to which peculiarities of human nature—to use this much defiled expression—should we ascribe those tendencies, that irresistible tropism toward finalities, that hope that some single supreme principle will be revealed to us that will explain the whole world and assume the burden of our existence, our behavior, and our thinking?

Various doctrines attempt to explain this yearning for self-definition by means of an absolute that exists outside ourselves, or what we may call a yearning for nonexistence. Through the ages theologians have tried to convince us that the Creator has imbued us with a natural gravitation toward Him that rules human thought; they call this natural religious feeling. It can certainly be called a justification of a doctrine through facts that can be accepted only by first accepting the doctrine. At any rate, why should we call religious feeling something that might just as easily manifest itself outside the realm of what we in daily life, as well as in science, call religion? Let us first define religion independently before we speak of *homo religiosus*; otherwise, as often happens, we may find ourselves defining religion in terms of religious feelings, and religious feelings in terms that posit a prior knowledge of what religion is. It is far simpler to examine religion as we know it from its historical formulations, as a particular instance of a broader phenomenon that can also occur outside religion.

But even if we discard the theological explanation, we still face a whole series of others that are merely different means of verbalizing the same thought and all of which, unfortunately, provoke so much doubt that they can scarcely be called explanations. Let us recall four such attempts:

One, formulated by Freud and abandoned by many of his disciples, is the theory of the death instinct, according to which there exists in living matter a constant nostalgia to return to a nonorganic state, a persistent tendency to lessen tensions and ultimately to liquidate them entirely—in other words, to bring about the atrophy of organic processes. The death instinct would thus be inimical to the libido yet could, at the same time, explain all the endeavors of the human mind to discover in the world principles that would reduce personal existence to impersonal forms.

The second doctrine has long been known in versions that are either methodological (Ockham), theological (Malebranche), or physical (De Maupertuis), and it has been clearly worked out as an economic principle by Avenarius and the empirio-critics. In its broadest metaphysical version this principle perceives in all nature—and thus in the behavior of organisms and in all thought —the continuous operation of the law of the maximal reduction of effort and the utilization of the simplest means. In this light, Freud's theory may be regarded as the application of the prin-

ciple of economy to the organic world. The principle of economy, as the natural striving of all systems to equalize tensions and differences, can also interpret the desire in man's thinking to reduce individuals to the undifferentiated absolute, to explain monistic realities.

The third possibility is the principle of simplification embodied in the "Gestalt" theory. According to this, all Gestalt systems or entities have an innate tendency to assume the simplest, most regular and symmetrical, least differentiated forms. This principle is a variation of the principle of economy and can be used for similar purposes.

In the fourth place we put Sartre's formula that existence "for itself," and thus human existence—defined as pure negativeness toward the rest of the world; as freedom, but freedom-*privatio* —nourishes a constant and contradictory wish to be transmuted into existence "in itself." It longs to discard its nothingness, which is a torment, but nothingness—freedom—is simultaneously what defines existence. Hence the wish to discard nothingness, to return to the world "in itself," is the wish to annihilate oneself as individual existence, and so to destroy existence itself.

All four of these explanations are, as we see, translations of the same thought into four different languages, and all provoke doubts and difficulties. Strictly speaking, they are attempts at a philosophic generalization of the principle of the growth of entropy. (The convergence of Wertheimer's and Köhler's "principle of pregnancy" and the principle of the growth of entropy is demonstrated by Wlodzimierz Szewczuk in his penetrating exposition of Gestalt psychology.) The theory of the death instinct and the principle of economy, as well as the other concepts we have discussed, are attempts to raise (or, we might say, lower) the principle of the growth of entropy to the level of a universal metaphysical thesis, applicable not only to known and hypothetical forms of energy, but to human behavior, emotions, and thought. If we were to accept this principle of a universal tendency to equalize tensions, to abolish asymmetry and differentiations, we could interpret the history of philosophy within its framework. All these variations of nostalgia for the

absolute that have filled philosophical life over the centuries would simply be separate instances of its action. The very essence of philosophical inquiries could then be deduced from this tendency which human thought shares with all other systems of energy. The content of the various metaphysical doctrines would be based on the processes of transformation of energy to which the human mind is subject; and the stubborn bond between philosophical conservatism on the one hand and social conservatism and the collective inertia we call reaction on the other, would also be a particular example of that principle.

However, if such a principle completely ruled human thinking, there could never have arisen that chronic conflict in philosophy which seems to dominate its written history: the conflict between a quest for the absolute and flight from it, between fear of oneself and fear of losing oneself in the very principle in which sustenance is hoped for. Thus thinking dominated by the growth of entropy, of conservatism, has been opposed in the course of intellectual history by a way of thinking that expresses the opposite, processes of increasing tension. All realms of culture, philosophy as much as art and custom, exemplify the paradox whereby everything that is new grows out of the endless need to question all existing absolutes. And though every new current of thought that tries to break away from acknowledged finalities establishes its own ultimates, and though every rebellion is therefore metamorphosed into a conservative state, still, it makes room for the next phase, where its own absolutes will in turn be the target of criticism. Can any method of thinking, even the most radical, escape this fate and resist the temptations of inertia throughout its history? All historical examples lead us to doubt it; indeed, the very hope of formulating such a method would be tantamount to the hope of achieving a final method, and thus precisely the kind whose nature would contradict its assumptions. The history of ancient skepticism provides us with an educational illustration: the doctrine whose premise was to question all dogmas, all that was obvious, was transformed into a barren, stony dogma of questioning for its own sake; criticism of the immobility of all ac-

cepted principles was converted into the immobility of universal criticism, for no principle of universal criticism can defend itself against the antinomy of the liar.

So we know of no completely flexible final method invulnerable to history's threat of petrifaction. We know only methods that maintain durable vitality because they have succeeded in creating tools of self-criticism, even though they may originally have included certain dogmatic premises or a belief in certain absolutes. We believe that several of these methods have, over a long period of time, devised instruments to overcome their own limitations. In our day Marxism, phenomenology, and psychoanalysis have demonstrated this radicalism. This statement does not mean, obviously, that we accept the disparate and contradictory propositions contained in these methods. It means that we recognize their capacity to transcend their own absolutes and detect the hidden premises of their own radicalism. From this stems their vitality and their continuity, not only as temples of true believers but also as thinking organisms capable of change. Though each of these doctrines contains a current of orthodoxy that can only repeat the original formulas without variation, each has produced, as well, offspring capable of life. The other "great doctrines" of the twentieth century, like Bergson's philosophy, never went beyond their initial phases and have remained in history as closed systems with admirers but no descendants.

The antagonism between a philosophy that perpetuates the absolute and a philosophy that questions accepted absolutes seems incurable, as incurable as that which exists between conservatism and radicalism in all aspects of human life. This is the antagonism between the priest and the jester, and in almost every epoch the philosophy of the priest and the philosophy of the jester are the two most general forms of intellectual culture. The priest is the guardian of the absolute; he sustains the cult of the final and the obvious as acknowledged by and contained in tradition. The jester is he who moves in good society without belonging to it, and treats it with impertinence; he who doubts all that appears self-evident. He could not do this if he belonged to good society; he would then be at best a salon scandalmonger. The jester must stand outside good society and observe it from the sidelines in order to unveil the nonobvious behind the obvious, the nonfinal behind the final; yet he must frequent society so as to know what it holds sacred and to have the opportunity to address it impertinently. Georges Sorel wrote about the jesting role of philosophy in connection with the encyclopedists, but in a pejorative sense. For him the jester was simply a toy of the aristocrats. But though it is true that philosophers have amused monarchs, their antics have played a part in earthquakes—precisely when they were the gambols of jesters. Priests and jesters cannot be reconciled unless one of them is transformed into the other, as sometimes happens. (Most often the jester becomes a priest—as Socrates became Plato—and not vice versa.) In every era the jester's philosophy exposes as doubtful what seems most unshakable, reveals the contradictions in what appears obvious and incontrovertible, derides common sense and reads sense into the absurd. In short, it undertakes the daily chores of the jester's profession together with the inevitable risk of appearing ridiculous. Depending on time and place, the jester's thinking can range through all the extremes of thought, for what is sacred today was paradoxical yesterday, and absolutes on the equator are often blasphemies at the poles. The jester's constant effort is to consider all the possible reasons for contradictory ideas. It is thus dialectical by nature— simply the attempt to change what is because it is. He is motivated not by a desire to be perverse but by distrust of a stabilized system. In a world where apparently everything has already happened, he represents an active imagination defined by the opposition it must overcome.

Fichte's great contribution was the simple observation that thought cannot move without obstacles, just as a car cannot start on ice or an airplane take off in a vacuum. For the same reason, any philosophy that is pure autoreflection or that is realized in the closed world of a monad is sheer delusion. And to suppose that the subject is identical with the object in the act of cognition is internally contradictory; to posit such an identity is tantamount to assuming immobility—a situation where no cognition can occur. If, then, philosophy undermines the absolute, if it rejects the uniform principles to which all reality can be reduced, if it confirms the pluralism of the world and the mutual nonreducibility of things, and at the same time affirms human individuality, it does not do so in the name of monadology or a concept of the individual as a self-sufficient atom. For human individuality can be upheld only in opposition to the rest of the world, that is, in its relations to the world—relations of dependence, responsibility, resistance.

A philosophy that tries to dispense with absolutes and with the prospect of finality cannot, by the nature of things, be a consistent structure, for it has no foundations and does not want a roof; it undermines existing structures and rips off existing roofs. In intellectual life it has all the vices and virtues of an indiscreet person with a stunted sense of respect. That is why in certain periods the conflict between the philosophy of the jester and that of the priest reminds us of the clash between the unbearable traits of adolescence and the equally unbearable traits of senility. The difference, of course, is that only the former are curable.

It is easy to see that all our reasoning up to this point can be suspected of falling prey to the monistic temptation it criticizes: the tendency to try to understand the multiplicity of facts by means of a single ordering principle. However, it is not the act of putting facts in order that is the opposite of anti-absolutist philosophy. Order can be a police slogan or the catchword of revolution. The opposite of an anti-absolutist philosophy is only a specific type of order, one that has put the whole multitude of existing and possible worlds into a unifying classification and is satisfied with the job. The police ideal is the order of a comprehensive file; philosophy's ideal is the order of an active imagination. The priest and the jester both violate the mind: the priest with the garrote of catechism, the fool with the needle of mockery. There are more priests than jesters at a king's court, just as there are more policemen than artists in his realm. Apparently it cannot be otherwise. The preponderance of believers in mythology over its critics seems inevitable and natural; it is the preponderance of a single world over the multiplicity of possible worlds, the preponderance of the ease of falling over the difficulty of climbing to the top. We observe this preponderance when we see the astonishing speed with which new mythologies displace old ones. In the intellectual life of a society in which the mechanism of traditional faith has become corroded, new myths proliferate with the greatest ease, even though they may originate in technical advancements or scientific discoveries. Thousands of people fondly imagine that the friendly inhabitants of other planets will one day solve the problems from which humans cannot extricate themselves. For others the word "cybernetics" embodies the hope of resolving all social conflicts. The rain of the gods falls from the heavens on the grave of the one God who has outlived himself. Atheists have their saints, and blasphemers build temples. Perhaps the longing for the absolute, the effort to equalize tensions, must fill an incomparably greater amount of space in the system than the growth of tensions, if the whole thing is to be kept from blowing sky-high. If this is so, then it explains why priests exist, though it is no reason for joining their ranks.

The priesthood is not simply a cult of the past seen through contemporary eyes, but a survival of the past intact in the present, an outgrowth of itself. It is not only a certain intellectual attitude toward the world, but a certain form of the world's existence—a factual continuation of a reality which no longer exists. In the attitude of the jester, on the contrary, a mere possibility materializes and becomes real in him before it exists in fact. For our thoughts about reality are also part of reality, no less important than other parts.

We declare ourselves in favor of the jester's philosophy, and thus vigilant against any absolute; but not as a result of a confrontation of arguments, for in these matters important choices are value judgments. We declare ourselves in favor of the possibilities contained in the extraintellectual values inherent in this attitude, although we also know its dangers and absurdities. Thus we opt for a vision of the world that offers us the burden of reconciling in our social behavior those opposites that are the most difficult to combine: goodness without universal toleration, courage without fanaticism, intelligence without discouragement, and hope without blindness. All other fruits of philosophical thinking are unimportant.

Karl Marx and the Classical Definition of Truth*

1. PRACTICAL ACTIVITY AND TRUTH: TWO CONCEPTS

The end of the nineteenth century gave birth to two different, though usually ill-differentiated, theories that tried to present man's practical activity as one of the principal categories of epistemological thinking. One of them, which we may call Marxism of a positivist orientation, is found in the philosophical writings of Engels. It invokes the *effectiveness* of human actions as a *criterion* with whose help it is possible and justifiable to *verify* the knowledge we need to undertake any sort of activity. The second, which found its classic though rather insouciant expression in the works of William James, introduces the concept of practical *usefulness* as a factor in the *definition* of truth. This usefulness is seen not as a tool for establishing the truth of man's knowledge independent of him, but as what *creates* this truth. Truth appears, therefore, to be relative to its application in daily life.

The two sets of terms that reveal the opposition between the theories are italicized. The first idea treats truth as the relation between a judgment or an opinion and the reality to which it refers; at the same time this relation is independent of man's knowledge of it. Man's practical activity does not create it, but merely ascertains its occurrence.

The role of man's practical activity as a criterion, and thus as a method of verification, depends on the active application of our knowledge in the hope of attaining a defined result. Success proves the truth of our knowledge, failure forces us to reject or modify it; and these measures do not at all involve the truth or falsity of

---

* This is an expanded version of a paper which the author read in December, 1958, at the University of Tübingen.

our judgment. If, for example, we are not certain today whether rational beings exist elsewhere in the solar system, nonetheless it is certain that the sentence "Rational beings are alive elsewhere than on the earth" is today either true or false. For judgments possess the property of relative truth or falseness independently of whether or not we know this property or are able to prove its existence. From this point of view the classical definition of truth remains completely valid, when we consider that any statement is in itself true or false on the necessary and sufficient condition that the reality of the thing or process it describes is as it states or not —and regardless of whether anyone has succeeded, or ever will, in establishing this through first-hand information or any other criterion. In this sense the relativity of truth is easily acceptable. It conforms to the concept of progress in human knowledge, in so far as this knowledge can ever succeed in formulating scientific generalizations to correspond accurately with their importance or applicability.

This doctrine, universally accepted in Marxist circles, was popularized, but also generalized, in Lenin's *Materialism and Empiriocriticism.* For Lenin thought it was possible to apply it not only to judgments but also to sense impressions, saying that they "copy," "photograph," or "reflect" the objects of the external world. These interpretations were not warmly welcomed by the positivists, and their cumbersome content had so many meanings as to be troublesome. Nevertheless, it would seem that with certain refinements they could be placed within the framework of the classical definition of truth that the Marxist tradition has relied on ever since Engels. It is obvious, in any case, that both Engels and Lenin saw the development of man's conceptual apparatus as an effort to copy ever more faithfully the external world, which was regarded as a pre-existing model. According to both, human cognition, though incapable of absolute and ultimate mastery of its object, approaches mastery by constant and progressive evolution. Its limitless striving for perfection is intended to make it more similar to reality, to make it imitate better the external world's properties and relations, which in themselves are independent of this effort and exist beyond the realm of human knowledge.

In the second of the two basic theories, man's practical activity has been elevated to the rank of an epistemological category, so that its functions are not limited to verification of the correspondence between human knowledge and a previously existing model, but are broadened to encompass the defining of the very concepts of truth, falseness, and nonsense.

We are not now trying to reconcile the various formulas that the pragmatists used to express their thinking—formulas that were frequently of dubious meaning and often seemingly or actually self-contradictory. Instead, let us limit ourselves to recalling the guideline that the first modern version of pragmatism left as its distinctive mark.

In this version—which as we know is not the sole form of pragmatism—the truth of a judgment is defined as a practical function of the usefulness of its acceptance or rejection. The meaning of a judgment is literally the same as the practical usefulness that the person who adopts this judgment derives from the influence that his acceptance of it has on his behavior. We can regard the judgment as true if as a result of accepting it our needs are better met or our position in life undergoes a positive change. We are likely to call this judgment false if its acceptance causes a lesser satisfaction of our needs or if the failure to realize some of our vital aspirations seems to stem from this acceptance.

From this doctrine it follows that, since its logical value is relative not only to the individual but, what is more, to the circumstances and moments in which it is expressed, a statement can turn out to be either true or false depending on the individual and on the sum total of needs that define his aspirations at a given time. To be true does not in the least mean to be in harmony with things that pre-exist as models to which our knowledge can be referred and compared; to be true means to fulfill the criterion of usefulness.

To apply criteria to a judgment is not, then, a way of verifying or establishing its truth, for that exists regardless. The act of application creates the truth or falseness of the judgment. Truth is not a report independent of its verification; the fact of its verification is simultaneously its act of birth. One can consider this theory of truth one of the possible formulations of idealism, if this doctrine is reducible to the thesis that all judgments, or at least all existential judgments, are meaningless unless one posits, implicitly or explicitly, a certain consciousness in reference to which this judgment is or is not valid.

In contrast to the theory provisionally described above as Marxism of a positivist orientation, the pragmatic concept of truth is clearly not compatible with the classical definition of truth. According to the first theory, human knowledge, though defined in its main lines by the biological and social needs of man, still hopes gradually to achieve an absolute copy of reality, which exists previously and always prior to cognition though it is capable of change. Knowledge is a means of satisfying human needs only to the extent that it is simultaneously an instrument which enables us to describe the world as it is "in itself." According to the second doctrine, cognition is a form of biological reaction that permits the best possible adaptation of individual organisms to their environment. Since the "classic" pragmatic concept of knowledge is purely biological, we can reasonably say that a given reaction of an organism to the stimuli of his environment is or is not adequate, is either useful or detrimental to the survival of the organism. Such evaluations are applicable to cognition as well; one can describe them from the same point of view and judge them true or false on the basis of results. But to ask if a given judgment is true or false in the current sense—if its essence is compatible with the world "in itself"—would be as futile as to ask if the reflex in the knee is true or false. It is hard to see what the "similarity" between objects and the content of knowledge could mean. But it is easy to understand the question whether the sum of biological reactions called cognition effectively serves to orient the organism in its environment, to satisfy its needs or innate instincts—the instinct of competition, for example, as in war or play.

If we can perceive in Engels' doctrine of the optimistic scientism that marked European intellectual life in the last decades of the nineteenth century, we are equally entitled to consider the first pragmatists advocates of the philosophy of individual success that for so long nourished the mind of the New World in its rapid economic development. One can find some of James's formulas duplicated almost literally in the writings of Henry Ford.

2. NATURE AS A PRODUCT OF MAN: MARX

These reflections are not new, of course, and their exposition would not be justified if this confrontation of two different visions of cognition—as a reflection of the world, and as an organic adaptation—did not aim to clarify the concept of cognitive man that I think exists in the writings of the young Marx, and that seems to grow out of sources and inspirations completely different from those that gave birth to contemporary Marxism.

These comments are based on the often-analyzed *Manuscripts* dated 1844, whose epistemological content seems to me as important as the general theory of man's alienation that most historians concentrate on. These texts, studied by many scholars for some years now, did not have a direct influence on the growth of dialectic thought, but after their publication they threw a new light not only on Marx's own intellectual development, but to an even greater degree on the relationship of contemporary Marxism to its original sources.

It seems to me that the vision of the world presented in the *Manuscripts* arises from an effort to consider man's practical activities as a factor that defines his behavior as a cognitive being. From the point of view of historical tradition, this attempt makes Marx's reflections similar to certain ideas contained in Spinoza's doctrine; analogous ideas were to appear in Bergson's analyses. (It is superfluous to stress that this strange "genealogy" is a purely conceptual construction and not in the strict sense a historical one.)

The basic point of departure for all of Marx's epistemological thought is the conviction that the relations between man and his environment are relations between the species and the objects of its need[1]; it also concerns the cognitive contact with things. Marx's thinking can be summarized in the following observations: 1. The world of things exists for man only as a totality of possible satisfactions of his needs.[2] 2. "And nature, conceived abstractly, in and of itself, perpetuated in its separation from man is nothing to him."[3] 3. If various objects, like the objects of science or art, are only a part of his consciousness, then in practice they are only a part of his life and his activity. Nature constitutes man's nonorganic flesh. 4. For Hegel, nature is the alienation of the consciousness, in view of which the conquering of alienation depends on the conquering of the very "object-ness" of the object; yet for Hegel it is not the "definiteness" of the object that creates the alienation, but its property of being an object.[4]

In this discussion we take as our point of departure one major theme of nascent Marxism: the idea of humanized nature. In what sense can nature—of which man, according to Marx, is unquestionably a product—be considered as the alienation of man or else as alienated man? Putting it another way, in what sense can man regard a part of nature as, in turn, a part of himself?

Existence "in itself" certainly cannot, according to this theory, be deduced from the data of consciousness. Yet existence "in itself" cannot be an object of cognition since it is not an object

---

1. In his notable study, *Le communisme* (1953), Dionys Mascolo considers Marxism from precisely this position, one in which man as a being with needs constitutes the point of departure. His is the best description I know of this aspect of Marx's doctrine.

2. Marx, *National Economy and Philosophy* (here and later I quote the text according to the edition *Marx, Early Writings*, Stuttgart, 1953, published by von Siegfried Landshut), p. 274: "Man is essentially a child of nature . . . the objects of his impulses exist outside him, independently, but these objects are necessary to him to allow him to bring his energies into operation and to affirm them, and are indispensable and significant. To say that man is a being that is corporeal, has natural strength, is alive, real, sentient, and objective means that real, material objects are the object of his being and of the expression of his life, or that he is capable of expressing his life only in relation to real, material objects."

3. *Ibid.*, p. 285.

4. See *ibid.*, p. 276.

of human activity. The assimilation of the external world, which is at first biological, subsequently social and therefore human, occurs as an organization of the raw material of nature in an effort to satisfy needs; cognition, which is a factor in the assimilation, cannot evade this universal determinism. To ask how an observer would see a world whose essence was pure thinking and consciousness of which was defined exclusively by a disinterested cognitive effort, is to ask a barren question, for all consciousness is actually born of practical needs, and the act of cognition itself is a tool designed to satisfy these needs. "The dispute about the reality or nonreality of thinking isolated from practice is purely scholastic." Nature appears as the opposition encountered by human drives, and all possible cognition is man's realization of the contact between conscious man and his awareness of external opposition. It is this contact which is the sole object man is capable of mastering intellectually. This means that it is fundamentally futile to hope that man by emancipating both elements of this relationship from himself can come to know the pure self, and thus himself as an independent consciousness, or else to know pure "externality," and thus existence in itself, which is not "given" to anyone though it is actually "given" and mirrored in that fancied contemplative consciousness.[5]

With this assumption, one can admit the validity of the idealists' traditional argument: "A situation in which one thinks of an object that is not thought of is impossible and internally contradictory." Still, it does not follow from this that to be "thought of" is the same thing as "to be." In addition, this argument does not describe adequately the relation between subject and object, because existence is really never "thought of" in the positivist or idealist sense. If existence can be the object of thought only as thought of existence—which is clearly tautological—then on the other hand, thought itself is a function of human existence and therefore of the practical behavior of the species. It is im-

---

5. It is thus that we permit ourselves to interpret Marx's remarks to the effect that the reality of any beings whatsoever is defined by the fact that they are both objects for others and have others as their objects (see *ibid.*, pp. 274–275).

possible for man to conceive of himself in his independence from nature, or of nature in its independence from his own practical contact with it or its opposition to his efforts, for it is this contact which gives birth to and defines his ability to comprehend. In this view, one's material situation depends on the conviction that the world of known phenomena, constituted as a field of man's social consciousness or as the force of opposition he feels, does not delimit the entire potential of opposition which human activity must overcome, that therefore the possibility of opposition not yet experienced always exists, and that in addition this experience of opposition constitutes and defines all consciousness.

If we now ask wherein lies that determination of the world through man's consciousness, of social existence carrying out its activity on recalcitrant material, we tend to see the answer in the reproach leveled against Hegel for treating object-ness itself, and not the definite character of the object, as a product of alienation. Thus for a certain object to be definite, in this sense, means that it possesses properties by which it can be differentiated from the rest of the world as an individual object. Still, it is impossible to comprehend the properties of any thing before one forms a general concept that can grasp this thing as in some respect similar to others, and thus also before one either creates a name to designate it or else is able to describe its properties with existing names. If things are not composed of their abstractly understood properties—if therefore it is impossible to recreate the individual out of a juxtaposition of a certain number of traits expressed in general terms—nevertheless it is equally true that only those general terms enable us to describe the individual. The world as it is conveyed to man's knowledge and as it is communicable in language is a world composed of abstractions; one arrives at the individual only through the intermediary of abstract and general concepts. Traditional empiricism, which presents cognition as the creation of concepts abstracted from individual observations of the properties of species, introduces the basic fact of consciousness: the indispensability of general knowledge to the perception of the concrete. Every thing as an object of cognition establishes the existence of man's conceptual apparatus, thanks to which one can differentiate that thing from the rest of the world. If the evolution of cognition strives toward an apprehension of the ever more abstract qualities of the world, then the perception of the concrete in a human way cannot dispense with either abstractions or generalities, both of which permit us to grasp this reality and also to describe it concretely, definitely, and specifically.

Human consciousness, the practical mind, although it does not produce existence, produces existence as composed of individuals divided into species and genera. From the moment man in his onto- and phylogenesis begins to dominate the world of things intellectually—from the moment he invents instruments that can organize it and then expresses this organization in words—he finds that world already constructed and differentiated, not according to some alleged natural classification but according to a classification imposed by the practical need for orientation in one's environment. The categories into which this world has been divided are not the result of a convention or a conscious social agreement; instead they are created by a spontaneous endeavor to conquer the opposition of things. It is this effort to subdue the chaos of reality that defines not only the history of mankind, but also the history of nature as an object of human needs—and we are capable of comprehending it only in this form. The cleavages of the world into species, and into individuals endowed with particular traits capable of being perceived separately, are the product of the practical mind, which makes the idea of opposition or even any kind of difference between it and the theoretical mind ridiculous.

Here is where Marxism differs from the Aristotelian conception of the world, or, more precisely, from Aristotelian realism, which posits that the species and genera into which the sciences divide reality are merely copies of the genera and species of this reality reflected more or less exactly, but ever more exactly, in the mirror of consciousness. "Humanized nature" knows no substantial forms inherent to itself or preceding human—that is, social—consciousness. This means that the forms appear as a result of man's intellectual organization of material, a task that is indispensable to organizing this material practically. Once people have enough free time to begin the task of epistemological reflection, the main results of this work are already prepared, and have been for a long time: this is the biological apparatus of human cognition. The habit of dividing the world in a definite way, selecting the components which correspond to requirements—for instance, those posed by the need for human survival—is an integral part of the most elementary activities of the human mind. We delude ourselves if we imagine that we perceive "sensuous qualities" as if they "were reflected" in our brains: "The eye has become the human eye, just as its object has become an object that is social, human, derived from man and destined for man. In this way, *the senses have become directly, in practice, theoreticians.*"[6] The qualities of things arise as human products, yet not in the idealist sense: if pure consciousness originally created them out of nothingness as immanent or at least wholly dependent on consciousness for their existence, in the same way as divine creativity, the existing world would be, from the theoretical point of view, even more difficult to understand than the theological world; it would also be even harder to justify its existence. (In fact, man has far fewer rational motives for creating a world *ex nihilo* than God has.)

Nor are the qualities of things forms or attributes of reality "in itself." They are "natural" to the degree that they are perpetuated in the substance given to man as the place of origin. They are subjective—or rather, socially subjective—as long as they bear the imprint of the organizational power of man, who sees the world in such terms and from such points of view as are necessary for him to adapt to it and to transform it usefully. Once we make this observation it is easy to see that the question of a picture of an absolutely independent reality is incorrectly posed: if such a picture were possible, man would no longer be possible.

This is one interpretation of "humanized nature" and of that material which divorced from man "is nothing" to him—the world presented in the writings of the young Marx. From the point of view of this anthropological, or anthropocentric, monism,

---

6. *Ibid.*, p. 240.

the picture of reality sketched by everyday perception and by scientific thinking is a kind of human creation (not imitation), since both the linguistic and the scientific division of the world into particular objects arise from man's practical needs. In this sense the world's products must be considered artificial. In this world the sun and stars exist because man is able to make them *his* objects, differentiated in material and conceived as "corporeal individuals." In abstract, nothing prevents us from dissecting surrounding material into fragments constructed in a manner completely different from what we are used to. (Thus, speaking more simply, we could build a world where there would be no such objects as "horse," "leaf," "star," and others allegedly devised by nature. Instead, there might be, for example, such objects as "half a horse and a piece of river," "my ear and the moon," and other similar products of a surrealist imagination. The surrealist world seems more "strange" to us than the usual one only because we do not have names for its components and do not use it in technology. Hence the human mind considers it "unreal" or else divides it into parts whose names it knows, thus preventing itself from perceiving it properly.) No division, not even the most fantastic as compared with what we are accustomed to, is theoretically less justified or less "true" than the one we accept in actuality. The problem is just that it is hard for us to imagine how such a world would appear, since it would be composed of objects we have no words to describe, and hence it would be inaccessible to our linguistic cognition.

What justifies our saying that the visual world of a fly, made up of light and dark spots of neutral colors, is less "authentic" or less "real" than ours, except the fact that ours is better adapted to our needs? True, we are able to reproduce the visual world of the fly in our sense apparatus, and the fly cannot do likewise with ours, for the fly's reality is not only different from but also poorer than the reality whose objective wealth, as we imagine, is at our disposal. It is not, though, for this reason less authentic. The whole of reality "in itself," being beyond our practical perception, is also beyond our knowledge. Its parts, its species—and thus also its properties, which allow it to submit to classification— have only an "*esse concessum*," an existence granted not as a result of an arbitrary convention, but as a result of a perceptual dialogue between man's work and the object's opposition to it. The components of language and thus the components of our cognition are also the components of the world. Language cannot be compared with a transparent glass through which one can contemplate the "objective" wealth of reality. It is a set of tools we use to adapt ourselves to reality and to adapt it to our needs—active tools, tools of construction, not of exploration.

This vision of the world does not in the least derive from a Kantian position; it does not proclaim that things as they are "in themselves" are inaccessible to the speculative mind, but rather that the question as posed by agnosticism is faulty. But if one could ask if "things as they are in themselves" can be revealed to the mind, one would first have to create an understandable concept of them. This is impracticable, however, for the very nature of concepts contradicts such an attempt. Only "things for us," not "things as they are in themselves," can have conceptual counterparts. Moreover, their existence comes into being simultaneously with their appearance as a picture in the human mind. Agnosticism might have a chance of success if it could succeed in formulating its question; its weakness lies in its inability to do so without a superfluity of words. It can verbalize the question, but it cannot convey any meaningful content; so, in the doctrine under consideration, one does not affirm something agnosticism denies, one rejects the question. Thus once again, "the dispute about the reality or nonreality of thinking isolated from practice is purely scholastic"; material divorced from man is nothing to him. In this sense, to ask about material "in itself" is to ask if nothingness exists; all possible replies lead to paralogisms, since the question postulates incorrectly constructed concepts.

It is true that one of Kant's basic ideas has been retained, the belief that the object cannot be conceived without the subject that constructs it. But the "subject" can be conceived only as a social subject, and "objects" are no longer contradistinct from a metaphysical world we know nothing of except that it exists and that it is not the world of material, since it is free from temporal and spatial determinants. Thus Marx's world could not be other than material since it poses an opposition to human endeavor. (Moreover, this explanation is tautological, for it is precisely this opposition that defines materiality as we understand it.) The speculative mind, whose various categories correspond to the objects of all possible experience, does not need to be complemented by a separate practical mind that would reveal the objects inaccessible to theoretical work to be moral postulates. For since the speculative mind is ruled by practicality, the objects it cannot comprehend, or the concepts that are "unconstruable" within its framework, cannot become accessible to a different, essentially practical cognitive power. In this situation one can find no differentiating criteria between the practical and the speculative mind.

As a result, there can exist no real, as opposed to imagined, problems that are basically unsolvable, for only questions in an understandable language can be formulated and considered; and questions about things or situations that are wholly unknown to us can be expressed only apparently. A question whose basic unsolvability was known to us would have to comprise, in one form or another, conceptual counterparts of objects that are unknowable directly. And in view of the reasons we have cited, such concepts cannot be formulated correctly.

As another result, it is difficult to imagine, from Marx's point of view, the possibility of an enduring, "pure," entirely universal and nonhistorical theory of knowledge—that is, of research into the cognitive capabilities of man in regard to the common and universal properties of human existence or else in regard to human nature in its immutable elements. One can investigate cognition only as history and analyze it not in its universality but in what is accessible to us in the transformations and interdependencies we know from history, from the social life of people and the mutable elements of their contact with nature, and from social conflicts and social groupings. A general theory of knowledge could be only the general awareness of this immutable situation; its role is therefore rather trivial. In other words, what is lasting in human nature is also the inviolable datum of all analysis and is the only state that can possibly be the starting point. We cannot weigh the influence of this "absolute" on our vision of the world. We can examine only what can undergo change; otherwise we would have to be able to shed our own skin and observe ourselves from outside. This is possible for the individual thanks to the existence of other individuals, but it is not possible for the social subject as a whole.

3. The Boundaries of Analogy

In order to state precisely, in several additional points, the hypothetical reconstruction of the vision of cognition which seems to emerge from Marx's observations, let us try to establish a certain line of demarcation to separate it from theories that are apparently or really akin to it.

When I evoked the name of Spinoza earlier I did not intend to launch into a discussion of the difficult question whether this philosopher's attempt at a comprehensive conception of the world could in effect, through the intermediary of Hegelian thought, have left its mark on the tendencies of nascent Marxism.[7] It was merely to note the striking convergence of the two, a convergence whose importance in the history of ideas goes beyond the limits of our deliberations. One of the most authentic characteristics of Spinoza's thinking is the opposition between a world conceived as a whole, and thus as a single substance, and a world composed of parts, and thus as a collection of separate modes. Metaphysical reality cannot be completely reconciled with any sort of division into parts. Acts of distinguishing between particular things, species, and individuals—quantitatively limited and qualitatively mutually differentiated—are maneuvers

---

7. Young Marx's contact with Spinoza occurred chiefly through the medium of Feuerbach, but this contact almost exclusively concerns matters linked with God, pantheism, and religious alienation. Although Spinoza's reflections on the integration of elements into the whole and of finished things into an unfinished thing do not have any general echo in Feuerbach's work, their pertinence to Hegelian logic is unquestionable.

that begin in a purely subjective realm defined by man's practical needs, and are done in response to the necessity of using things in daily life. A world thus divided also constitutes a field of activity for science, and its results, though extremely profitable for the human species, have nothing in common with the need for a disinterested contemplation of reality. Such contemplation, liberating itself from the images imposed by imagination and experience, succeeds to the degree that the thinker manages to penetrate that indivisible whole of substance by an effort that ends in total identification with his object. The theoretical mind cannot be separated from the practical mind; the theoretical mind is the surgeon who cuts the indivisible whole of reality into disparate fragments accessible to human operations. It is possible to conceive of any individual finished object only thanks to abstract work, for the mutual bonds and reactions of things, their universal "concatenation," make every fragment of reality identical, literally speaking, with the whole. The so-called concrete must therefore be considered a product of an abstraction that owes its existence to the distorting perception of man. This perception is an abstraction precisely because it is empirical—it takes as its point of departure particular individuals, the objects of the senses. In reality only the cosmos as a whole is concrete in the true sense, and all the parts are fictitious abstractions created to satisfy the requirements of everyday life, not of a disinterested examination.

This view of the world is but one of the themes we find in that heterogeneous work which is Spinoza's. We need not try to prove the accuracy of its interpretation, but discernible in it is the essential idea hypothetically posed as the basis of young Marx's epistemology, the idea that nature is composed of separate parts and that species are an "artificial" creation arising from the practical needs of man and from his effort to master nature. In other words, this is an extreme statement of Platonism, if it is correct to sum up the essence of that philosophy as the affirmation that there exists a natural classification of the world.

But it is only up to this point that the analogy holds. An integral component of Spinoza's thought is the conviction that this

practical determination of normal intellectual work and of everyday imagination renders them both incapable of an authentic
knowledge of reality; that, on the other hand, there exists aside
from them, or rather beyond them, the instrument of intuitive
knowledge free from the distortions that are inevitable in the
activity of the theoretical mind. Spinoza's intuition, in at least
one version (I think there are more than one, and mutually
contradictory at that), carries out in a different fashion the work
of Kant's practical mind: it permits us to penetrate reality "in
itself," hidden behind the deformed images of the imagination
and the empirical sciences. Now the second, enigmatic world
remains for Marx reduced to nothingness and rejected except for
questions that can be formulated intelligibly. One is tempted
to say that this is a human nothingness just as the reality in which
we live is human, that the act of creating the object "for us"
becomes identical with the act of destroying the object "in itself."
In this sense one can say that Marxist metaphysics is impossible.
If by definition one ascribes to metaphysics the property of being
a knowledge of the world absolutely independent of all human
coefficients, then it is evident that from Marx's point of view
it would have to be considered as necessarily internally contradictory, since these coefficients cannot be eliminated from cognition. That is why Marxism, thus understood, cannot set itself
a program of transcendental metaphysics conceived either as an
intellectual enterprise yielding results in the form of linguistic
knowledge, or as a purely intuitive effort climaxed by its integration into or its identification with the reality whose root it seeks.

If a renunciation of the deceptive pictures produced by a cognition that imitates reality "in itself" differentiates Marx's epistemology from ideas that are positivistically or scientistically inspired, then the rejection of knowledge that assimilates reality
in an act of intuitive integration undermines a possible analogy
with Bergson's thinking. In the latter, which we need not go
into now, we find the same Spinozan desire to overcome the
limitations and distortions inevitably imposed on us by discursive
cognition—to shed this cognition precisely because of its practical origins for the sake of a disinterested inquiry into truth.

Marx rejects the antithesis between the world shaped into a human image and the world pre-existing "in itself" that one seeks to grasp in a futile effort to conquer oneself as a man. That is why, from Marx's viewpoint, it would be pointless to stigmatize this cognition by calling it "distorted"; even if we remove the pejorative aura from the word, distortion could be proved only through a model with which to compare the "distorted" picture—an impracticable assignment, for the world as given to the human species is absolute. We do not have the right to suppose that pre-existent reality bears the qualities of man's reality, nor have we the tools to plumb nature and the kind of distortions it undergoes when it abandons its transcendency to display itself to us. Without denying its existence or declaring it unknowable, we reject it as a possible object of research. Let us add that Marx never considered that human knowledge, no matter how incapable of liberating itself from its limitations by means of intuitive vision, was doomed to create a picture of reality that was inescapably mechanistic.

We need not stress that Marxist epistemology, thus reconstructed, reveals that its supposed consanguinity with such voluntaristic doctrines as the theory of Maine de Biran, later reviewed by Wilhelm Dilthey, is superficial. Here no act of pure will is raised to the rank of a primal fact of consciousness. Active contact with the opposition of nature creates at one and the same time conceptive man and nature as his object. No epistemological absolute exists, either as reality in itself which "is reflected" in consciousness, or as a sense impression, or a *cogito*, or innate categories of the mind, or pure nonpsychic phenomena. The only accessible world that exists is the endless conflict between social man's needs and the natural environment as the possible means of satisfying them. In this process there is nothing we can interpret as fixed and elementarily obvious, eluding all further control and demanding that we accept it as a "primal fact." Nor is there any epistemological analysis that can enable us to distribute the contents of our knowledge over primary elements, the indivisible and unverifiable atoms of consciousness.

Still, it would be dangerous to push this elucidation too far while simultaneously maintaining that it is completely contained or preformed in Marx's thought. We know, of course, that we are spinning out suppositions based on unfinished and not unequivocal texts. An overdetailed interpretation of aphorisms runs the risk of letting us ascribe to their author statements that might well surprise him. Therefore it is only in terms derived from our own reconstruction that we will discuss the difference between Marxist epistemology and the two doctrines related to it in the domain of the concept of truth, as well as the so-called classical definition of the word itself.

As a matter of fact, we discover in this theory a tendency which brings it close to the thinking of the pragmatists, and which deserves our attention despite the opposition between the two doctrines. Both manifest the same hostility toward any theory that holds consciousness to be an ever more perfect imitation of an external model that acts on the mind through some sort of "species" imprinted upon the sensory organs and that introduces into the mind an ever more exact replica of reality.

Instead, as we see, both conceive of cognition as essentially functional; a tool that permits man to master the circumstances of his life, not a photographic plate that reproduces the pictures it receives. Practical activity defines man's consciousness not only as a selective factor that steers his interest toward one or another object of the world, not only as an instrument of control that permits us to verify the knowledge we have gained, but above and beyond all as a tool with which man can introduce into matter a definite system of intellectual organization.

If it is correct, from Marx's point of view, to say that consciousness is things represented, then it is even more accurate to summarize his thought by saying that things are consciousness made concrete. The first statement concerns only the origins of consciousness in the contacts of the human species with the opposition of its environment taken as a whole, or as a preexisting "chaos"; the second takes into consideration the world of things already shaped and differentiated from each other. The first of the two worlds is the primal *universum* "in itself"—the Spinozan substance. The second is composed of objects of different qualities organized in species, and thus in collectives perpetuated in human thought and speech.

The existence of this "chaos" is not unimportant for epistemology; it is what defines the opposition between the Marxist and the pragmatist theories of knowledge. Truth conceived as a relationship of "resemblance" between human judgments and a wholly independent reality is unacceptable to a Marxist picture of the world. Nonetheless, truth does not depend exclusively on a relationship of biological correspondence, that is to say, on the relationship between judgment and its practical utility for the individual. Given this last assumption, we are obliged to admit that reality is not only wholly produced *ex nihilo* for each separate individual, but that this act of production must be renewed at every moment for that individual. For it is also possible and probable that a judgment recognized as true in a given moment on the basis of the criterion of utility can become useless a moment later, and thus nonsensical or even harmful as well as false.

Pragmatist relativism—in which these formulas, though perhaps extreme, are nevertheless inexorably implied if we take James's "classical" pronouncements seriously and literally—is irreconcilable with Marx's thought for two major reasons. The first is the impossibility of creating *ex nihilo*; the second, the impossibility of conceiving human consciousnes as a social instrument irreducible to the behavior of particular organisms. That is why reality is neither a complex of phenomena whose existence some individual recognized at a particular moment as useful nor the sum total of an individual's conscious response to the stimulus of his needs. There exists a reality that is common to all people and that remains forever in a state of incipience, a reality in which the phenomenon of creativity certainly occurs but in which a certain constant is retained that corresponds to what we can call "human nature" or else to that totality of human properties, biological needs, and social relations which can rightfully be termed immutable. The concept of human nature retains its validity to the degree that the concept of enduring reality as an epistemological category is justified—reality accessible to man, therefore the only one worthy of being taken into consideration. To this reality one can also apply the Aristotelian concept of truth. The compatibility of judgment with reality is no longer a relationship of "resemblance" between this judgment and the world "in itself"; it applies to that world upon which man has already imposed "substantial forms."

The classical definition of truth then assumes a sense which is not entirely classical; in essence, by retaining unchanged its traditional meaning and its traditional intention, we establish a vital part of Aristotelian metaphysics, the belief that the entire apparatus of human language that describes reality according to defined categories has its exact corollaries in reality itself, and that therefore the forms, the by-products, and all the properties of reality are perpetuated in things just as they are in language. On the other hand, in supposing that the reality which our language divides into species is born at the same time as language itself, we simultaneously suppose that the relations between things, whose description is called true or false, are relations between "artificial" objects carved out of material according to a system of partition that renders reality malleable to human practice. The subjects and predicates of judgments (if we limit our observation to them) to which one assigns logical value—conformity or nonconformity with reality—must be names of things that are absolutely independent, if truth or falsity in the traditional sense is to be applied to them. Individuals and species thus exist in material itself just as they exist in words—moreover, the species of reality exist not only in nouns and adjectives, but also in verbs and other parts of speech.

If, for Marx, man replaces God-the-Creator, still He is not the God of Augustine or Thomas Aquinas, a God who gives birth to the world out of nothingness; rather, He reminds us of the God of the Averroists, who organizes the world out of previously existing material. Once created, this world becomes the only one, and the act of creation annihilates the primal chaos. But awareness of this situation does not lead to positive atheism, the conviction that God does not exist: "Atheism as a negation of this dependence [man's] loses its meaning, for it is the *negation of*

God and affirms, by this negation, the existence of man; but socialism as such no longer needs this intermediary. . . . It is the *positive self-knowledge* of man which is no longer conditioned upon the abolition of religion, just as *real life* is the positive reality of man no longer conditioned upon the abolition of private property, i.e., communism."[8]

The difference between material objects, which man creates, and God, whom he also creates, becomes a functional difference: the existence of God becomes a form of human captivity, for God is a thing that man cannot adapt to himself—and this develops from the fact that there are some things man cannot adapt to himself. Awareness liberated from alienation, according to Marx, abolishes God in abolishing atheism—in refusing to reply to the traditional question: Was the world created by someone outside? The disclosure that the world is a human product is actually an act of that social quasi-*cogito* which requires no justification via additional reasons, for it is not a theoretical thesis but a state of social consciousness that confirms its own autonomy; thus liberty, once achieved, does not need to justify itself. It can defend itself against threats, but the search for self-justification is up to those who threaten it.

4. HISTORICAL COGNITION

I need not go further into a discussion of the Marxist theory of alienation, of analyses of the situation of man who has lost control over the world he himself called into being. In this epistemology, or rather this embryo of an epistemology—which I think is not only found in Marx's thought, but is also philosophically worthy of continuation—there exist certain points which require clarification. Two of them are especially significant.

The first concerns the continuous character of the creation of the world in cognition, and above all its prolongation in historical cognition.

We observed above that according to this epistemology the relativity of cognition is limited by the constant human coefficient that

8. *Marx, Early Writings*, p. 248.

introduces into reality certain constant divisions as correlatives of the permanent elements of human nature, and that the reality which is immutable (on the scale of human history, obviously) is conceivable to the degree to which there exist immutable human needs and relations. This constant, which constitutes the primary material of our cognition, and thus everything that seems unquestionably "natural" (like the material objects of everyday life), does not by any means comprise the entire object of cognition. The creation of the world, bound to the peculiarities of man as such, precedes the creative activities and later deformations attendant upon all the mutable components of history: epochs, social classes, political situations, national sentiments—all that research includes in the sociology of knowledge. We cannot imagine how the humanized nature of the world could be overcome by the cognition of the man who shaped it. Instead, we sometimes believe that we are capable of liberating ourselves completely from all the ingredients of a world-view imposed by mutable historical conditions, or else that an image of the world that is absolutely objective (within the limits drawn by immutable "human nature") is possible. This question has been discussed through the ages, especially in reference to the cognition of human historical reality.

Thus it would seem possible here to take the same point of view that Marx holds in weighing the matter of cognition in general. In other words, one can consider historical cognition as a function of the tasks imposed on the scholar by *his epoch*. These tasks force him to slice up historical material and to select conceptual tools applicable to it according to value criteria supplied by his times and his specific environment. For example, in the history of ideas we always find a considerable number of different interpretations of the same collection of facts, interpretations that can be coherent and indisputable and that moreover show themselves capable of a satisfactory explanation of all the phenomena under examination. Often, too, the historian of ideas attributes to past thinkers answers to questions that they surely never posed to themselves, but that seem to him important from the point of view of his age. This is not surprising, indeed it is inevitable if the historical sciences are to exist. Considering that the historian of ideas always tries both to understand and interpret known facts and to reveal hitherto hidden facts, considering also that various competing interpretations of these facts can be justified, it is an illusion to hope that some absolutely definitive interpretation can be established once and for all. Certainly there are technical criteria that make one interpretation outweigh another. For instance, it is incontestable that an interpretation that permits us to explain the maximum number of facts is *ceteris paribus* more worthy of acceptance. Some interpretations dispense with confronting all the facts under consideration (for example, all the texts of a given author), whereas others offer a choice. Some use methodological rules whose fruitfulness has been demonstrated in other fields; others are suspect because they are contradictory; and so on. Even the most rigorous technical criteria, if they allow us to eliminate interpretations that are fantasies or caricatures, still do not permit us to destroy summarily the entire range of varied and contradictory interpretations of the same sum total of facts. This variety, of course, is precisely what enables the historical sciences to exist at all.

The probability that some unknown texts of Plato will yet come to light is rather small, but it is undoubtedly true that Plato's thought, as presented in existing texts, will never cease to be analyzed in different ways and will be subject to the most varied interpretations; and no version that is absolutely final, conclusive, and invulnerable will ever succeed in establishing itself for all time. It happens thus with all historical work that progresses without basing itself on the discovery of hitherto unknown data. This is understandable when we consider that the questions we pose today, those that are imposed on us by our own situation, we also pose to past thought, which never asked them of itself, for the combination of concepts we use to study a problem has been formed in our own era and by a different process.

It is obvious that in posing such questions as, Is the Cartesian *cogito* an act of thinking of something outside man or an act of pure self-knowledge? Is Thomas Moore's utopia a Christian institution?—we answer by using a method completely different from the one we use with questions such as: Was Siger de Brabant murdered by his opponents in the Church or not? How long did Duns Scotus teach in Paris? In the first instance, though one can always find data supporting one or another reply, and though the questions are not entirely pointless, nevertheless we realize that these writers probably did not pose these questions to themselves, and in any event did not pose them in the same way. Therefore the scholar does not so much discover answers as mold them for his authors from the material they have supplied. His conceptual apparatus is different, and so is the hierarchy of values he ascribes to problems. The *découpage* he performs on the object of his studies is therefore never "natural," that is, compatible with what the author in question wrote; it is imposed by the tools used, and in that sense is artificial. However, it is not necessarily false, since an interpretation is false only when the technical rules of research are not observed, and certainly the most important rule is the one that requires an explanation of the greatest possible amount of data.

In its relationship to its material the science of the history of ideas then finds itself in the same situation as that of the human species vis-à-vis the world: unable to create the world *ex nihilo*, historiography imposes its limited system of divisions and makes a choice among factors which it tends unconsciously to judge as differentiated, in this or some other way, according to their pertinence. This is a simple statement of fact, not an expression of intent to see history as a projection of the present into the past. The intentional application of such a rule risks shocking distortions, and in any case provides disastrous justifications for arbitrary choices of facts and for the ignoring of facts incompatible with a previously accepted hypothesis. This changeable system of divisions we are speaking about is a function of conditions that the researcher never defines according to his own will—as opposed to a painter, for example, who can never be accused of painting false pictures. If, therefore, we can reasonably say that the historian like the painter creates objects which do not exist in "nature," still the former is always bound by the principle of noncontradiction toward known data, whereas the latter does not bear this responsibility, though he knows the material from which he ultimately produces his world. It is also certain that there are limits to the similarity between scientific historical creativity and the creativity that the human species as a whole exerts on its material "substance." The conditions that limit a historian's use of a conceptual apparatus in the analysis of his object change not only depending on historical eras, but also on different views of the world which in the same era create different environments, classes, and social groups.

If, then, the countless different pictures of the same collection of facts co-exist and if all are approximately compatible with accepted technical rules of scholarly work, then the choice among them is defined by a more general choice, one of a certain view of the world, which constitutes an integral part of historical interpretation. Since it seems inevitable that in different pictures of the world some factors are always in the strict sense unverifiable (which does not mean that all these pictures are irrational to the same degree), we must note that at a given point in an analysis it is difficult to characterize the next choice as an option between "truth" and "falsehood." It is a choice of positions and not of theoretical theses; practical, not speculative. Thus it is unreasonable to hope that total "objectivity" can be introduced, once and for all, into historical knowledge. We do not mean to renounce the effort to broaden in every possible degree the role of rational factors in philosophical and historical constructions, nor the possibility of finding another adjective for statements that we cannot evaluate as "true" or "false" in the usual sense. In the eventualities we are speaking of, it is no longer a matter of a choice between two logical values, but simply between two values.

5. COGNITION OF VALUES

This is the place for a second observation that was implied above: that it is impossible to deduce sound value judgments from so-called descriptive judgments, and that the former are never logically equivalent to the latter. This is a truth that has been very well demonstrated over the ages, particularly by thinkers of a positivist orientation. Recognizing the heterological character of the world of values and the world of things in human cognition, we still think that in the light of Marxist epistemology the mere statement is not enough to give us a knowledge of the degree and nature of this heterology or of the range of possible applications of the criteria of truth and falsehood.

It follows from our previous observations that according to Marx, the choice between values—or rather, since it is not a matter of intentional and voluntary acts, of preferences determined by practical considerations—constitutes an inevitable part of human cognition. In other words, the things our world is composed of are things that are selected since they are created, in the sense we have given to this word. Thus it would seem that the acceptance of certain established values is inevitable in our every act of cognition, which might lead us to suppose that the difference we have cited between the two possible forms of intellectual assimilation of the world is nonexistent. In reality, we see that the difference does exist when we consider that the evaluations, or rather the practical positions, involved in human cognition not only need not be conscious to exert their influence, but have taken on the shape of an enduring *habitus* peculiar to man as such, and thus are historically immutable. For this reason, too, there is no need to take them into consideration at all in intellectual work.

These positions, common to the whole human race, have made our external world as it is, permanent in its basic partitions. The values and practical preferences we have put into this world are concealed within it; we no longer see the mark we have stamped upon the world and upon its permanent human coefficient. This seal is born and dies with man: there is no reason why he should retain a distinct consciousness of it. This world can be considered as given, since no other exists and since everything we have added to it and molded within it has, for us, become petrified in a quasi-in-itself reality. This is not so in the case of those practical positions and preferences which change in the course of human history, whose transformations are clearly obvious to man and which divide the species into classes, nations, professions, sexes, generations, personalities, particular situations in life—in short, everything that in any way influences the sum of values each of us tends to prefer over others. It is evident that this world of values is not created automatically by the world of things which is common to almost everyone and in which habits common to the whole species are involved. A description of this first world, or rather of these many worlds (therefore, value judgments), cannot be deduced from the description of the second (therefore, from judgments of fact, to use this awkward noun). In this sense, the objection of the positivists is justified.

Let us bypass the huge mass of questions, discussed over the ages and still controversial, connected with this famous objection. Yet let us say that we cannot be satisfied with the mere statement that these two worlds are epistemologically nonhomogeneous for the same reason we formulated in regard to historical cognition, and which we can broaden to include cognition of the human world in general. In all cognition there exist in essence factors irreducible to judgments of fact, or let us say to theoretical statements; for this is not a matter of individual statements, to which the natural sciences are also not reducible, but of "speculative" cognition. Putting it another way, aside from everything that can be studied and verified by the application of technical rules, there exist in this cognition factors imposed by a general view of the world, where practical preferences and attitudes inevitably decide the questions to which there are no means of supplying scientifically based replies—that is, where those technical rules are impotent to judge positions. In the cognition of the human world—in the fields of sociology, of the history of ideas, the history of culture, and so on—it is impossible to avoid choices defined by values, which does not necessarily mean that these choices are completely arbitrary, unconditioned, or simply dependent upon the free will of the individual. This observation does not permit us to raise value judgments to the level of theoretical judgments, but it does bring their logical situation closer to that of a certain important field of knowledge, namely, knowledge of the world that is essentially human.

Consequently, we can assume that in the confrontations and controversies of different normative systems we are not logically

much worse off than in the case of disputes about generalizations
in many humanistic sciences, although in the latter we rarely explicitly invoke values to prove the correctness of our positions.
Comparing the quantity of practical hazards and practical reasons
that determine controversial choices in the humanities to the
same factors involved in the natural sciences (we are concerned,
obviously, with the substance of the reply and not the selection
of an object of research), we are inclined to believe that the division between these two realms of scientific knowledge is deeper
than between cognition of values and what we usually call scientific cognition in general—if it is a matter of the role of the
practical reasons involved in the acceptance of some hypothesis
or some value. Daily observation of disputes in these fields seems
to substantiate this belief. We do not, consequently, exclude the
possibility of an epistemology in which cognition of values will
draw nearer to theoretical cognition as a result of a more detailed
analysis of the ideological character of humanistic knowledge.

This attempt to explain what is in our opinion the basic principle of Marx's epistemology has led us to a simple conclusion:
Nascent Marxism formulated a germinal project for a theory of
cognition that in the course of the development of the current
of thinking that identifies itself as Marxist was replaced by the
radically different concepts of Engels and especially Lenin. (I
say "especially," having in mind the extreme formulations that
Lenin used to characterize his theory of reflection—of consciousness that copies and imitates reality.) We need not try to analyze
all the reasons that led to this peculiar evolution, but there are
certainly several. (In Engels' case it is obviously difficult to exclude the influence of the positivist scientism widespread in his
day; in Lenin's, the influence of the tradition of Russian materialism; and after all, these only partly explain the matter.)

What is also evident when one studies Marx's *Manuscripts* is
the links he himself established between his concept of cognition,
his "denaturalization" of the world, and the idea of the abolition
of human alienation through communist society. And though
there is nothing easier today than to demonstrate how very

utopian was Marx's conviction that "communism as the positive abolition of private property" is identical with the abolition of human alienation in general,[9] still we can believe that his epistemological point of departure did not merely for this reason become philosophically sterile. We know, too, the analogous ideas —enmeshed in various contexts and therefore also endowed with various meanings—that arose completely independently of the Marxist tradition among many philosophers.

It is probable in any event that a certain method of analyzing human cognition, in everyday perception as well as in art and science, could be worked out upon precisely this basic idea of Marx: that man as a cognitive being is only part of man as a whole; that that part is constantly involved in a process of progressive autonomization, nevertheless it cannot be understood otherwise than as a function of a continuing dialogue between human needs and their objects. This dialogue, called work, is created by both the human species and the external world, which thus becomes accessible to man only in its humanized form. In this sense we can say that in all the universe man cannot find a well so deep that, leaning over it, he does not discover at the bottom his own face.

---

9. *Ibid.*, pp. 235–236.

The Concept of the Left

Every work of man is a compromise between the material and the tool. Tools are never quite equal to their tasks, and none is beyond improvement. Aside from differences in human skill, the tool's imperfection and the material's resistance together set the limits that determine the end product. But the tool must fit the material, no matter how remotely, if it isn't to produce a monstrosity. You cannot properly clean teeth with an oil drill or perform brain operations with a pencil. Whenever such attempts have been made the results have always been less than satisfactory.

THE LEFT AS NEGATION

Social revolutions are a compromise between utopia and historical reality. The tool of the revolution is utopia, and the material is the social reality on which one wants to impose a new form. And the tool must to some degree fit the substance if the results are not to become ludicrous.

There is, however, an essential difference between work on physical objects and work on history; for the latter, which is the substance, also creates the tools used to give this substance shape. Utopias which try to give history a new form are themselves a product of history, while history itself remains anonymous. That is why even when the tools turn out to be grossly unsuited to the material, no one is to blame, and it would be senseless to hold anyone responsible.

On the other hand, history is a human product. Although no individual is responsible for the results of the historical process, still each is responsible for his personal involvement in it. Therefore each is also responsible for his role in fashioning the intellectual tools used upon reality in order to change it—for accepting or rejecting a given utopia and the means employed to realize it.

To construct a utopia is always an act of negation toward an existing reality, a desire to transform it. But *negation is not the opposite of construction—it is only the opposite of affirming existing conditions.* That is why it makes little sense to reproach someone for committing a destructive rather than a constructive act because every act of construction is necessarily a negation of the existing order. At most, you may reproach him for not supporting the reality that exists and for wanting to change it; or, on the other hand, for accepting it without qualification, without seeking change; or, finally, for seeking harmful changes. But a negative position is only the opposite of a conservative attitude toward the world, negation in itself being merely a desire for change. The difference between destructive and constructive work lies in a verbal mystification stemming from the adjectives used to describe the changes, which are considered either good or bad. Every change is, in fact, an act both negative and positive at one and the same time, and the opposite only of an affirmation of things as they are. To blow up a house is just as constructive as to build one—and at the same time just as negative. Of course, this does not mean that it is all the same whether one destroys or builds a house. The difference between the two acts is that the first, in most instances, works to the detriment of the people involved, and the second is almost always to their benefit. The opposite of blowing up a house is not to build a new house but to retain the existing one.

This observation will serve to lead to conclusions whose aim is to define more closely the meaning we give to the concept of the social Left.

The Left—and this is its unchangeable and indispensable quality, though by no means its only one—is a movement of negation toward the existent world. For this very reason it is, as we have seen, a constructive force. It is, simply, a quest for change.

That is why *the Left rejects the objection that its program is only a negative and not a constructive one.*

The Left can cope with reproaches directed at the potential harm or utility that may arise from its negations. It can also contend with the conservative attitude that wants to perpetuate things as they are. It will not defend itself, however, against the accusation of being purely negative, because every constructive program is negative, and vice versa. A Left without a constructive program cannot, by that token, have a negative one, since these two terms are synonymous. If there is no program, there is at the same time no negation, that is, no opposite of the Left—in other words, conservativism.

UTOPIA AND THE LEFT

But the act of negation does not in itself define the Left, for there are movements with retrogressive goals. Hitlerism was the negation of the Weimar Republic, but this does not make it leftist. In countries not controlled by the Right, an extreme counterrevolutionary movement is always a negation of the existing order. Thus the Left is defined by its negation, but not only by this; it is also defined by the direction of this negation, in fact, by the nature of its utopia.

I use the word "utopia" deliberately and not in the derogatory sense that expresses the absurd notion that all social changes are pipe dreams. By utopia I mean a state of social consciousness, a mental counterpart to the social movement striving for radical change in the world—a counterpart itself inadequate to these changes and merely reflecting them in an idealized and obscure form. It endows the real movement with the sense of realizing an ideal born in the realm of pure spirit and not in current historical experience. Utopia is, therefore, a mysterious consciousness of an actual historical tendency. As long as this tendency lives only a clandestine existence, without finding expression in mass social movements, it gives birth to utopias in the narrower sense, that is, to individually constructed models of the world, as it should be. But in time utopia becomes actual social consciousness; it invades the consciousness of a mass movement and becomes one of its essential driving forces. Utopia, then, crosses over from the domain of theoretical and moral thought into the field of practical thinking, and itself begins to govern human action.

Still, this does not make it realizable. Utopia always remains a phenomenon of the world of thought; even when backed by the power of a social movement and, more importantly, even when it enters its consciousness, it is inadequate, going far beyond the movement's potentials. It is, in a way, "pathological" (in a loose sense of the word, for utopian consciousness is in fact a natural social phenomenon). It is a warped attempt to impose upon a historically realistic movement goals that are beyond history.

However—and this is fundamental to an understanding of the internal contradictions of left-wing movements—the Left cannot do without a utopia. The Left gives forth utopias just as the pancreas discharges insulin—by virtue of an innate law. Utopia is the striving for changes which "realistically" cannot be brought about by immediate action, which lie beyond the forseeable future and defy planning. Still, utopia is a tool of action upon reality and of planning social activity.

A utopia, if it proves so remote from reality that the wish to enforce it would be grotesque, would lead to a monstrous deformation, to socially harmful changes threatening the freedom of man. The Left, if it succeeds, would then turn into its opposite —the Right. But then, too, the utopia would cease to be a utopia and become a slogan justifying every current practice.

On the other hand, the Left cannot renounce utopia; it cannot give up goals that are, for the time being, unattainable, but that impart meaning to social changes. I am speaking of the social Left as a whole, for though the concept of the Left is relative— one is a leftist only in comparison with something, and not in absolute terms—still the extreme element of every Left is a revolutionary movement. The revolutionary movement is a catch-all for all the ultimate demands made upon existing society. It is a total negation of the existing system and, therefore, also a total program. A total program is, in fact, a utopia. A utopia is a necessary component of the revolutionary Left, and the latter is a necessary product of the social Left as a whole.

Yet why is a utopia a condition of all revolutionary movements? Because much historical experience, more or less buried in the social consciousness, tells us that goals unattainable now will never be reached unless they are articulated when they are still unattainable. It may well be that the impossible at a given moment can become possible only by being stated at a time when it is impossible. To cite an example, a series of reforms will never attain the goals of revolution, a consistent reform party will never imperceptibly be transformed into the fulfillment of a revolution. *The existence of a utopia as a utopia is the necessary prerequisite for its eventually ceasing to be a utopia.*

A revolutionary movement cannot be born simultaneously with the act of revolution, for without a revolutionary movement to precede it the revolution could never come about. As long as the revolutionary act has not been accomplished, or is not indisputably and clearly evident, it is a utopia. For today's Spanish proletariat a social revolution is a utopia; but the Spanish proletariat will never achieve a revolution if it does not proclaim it when it is impossible. This is why tradition plays such an important role in the revolutionary movement: the movement would never know any victories if it had not in previous phases suffered inevitable defeats—if it had not initiated revolutionary activity when the historical situation precluded success.

The desire for revolution cannot be born only when the situation is ripe, because among the conditions for this ripeness are the revolutionary demands made of an unripe reality. The continuous influence of social consciousness is one of the necessary conditions for the maturation of history to the point of radical change; utopia is a prerequisite of social upheavals, just as unrealistic efforts are the precondition of realistic ones. That is the reason why revolutionary consciousness cannot be satisfied with mere participation in changes already taking place; it cannot merely follow events, but must precede them at a time when they are neither planned nor anticipated.

Therefore—and this is an elementary practical conclusion— *the Left doesn't mind being reproached for striving for a utopia.* It may have to defend itself against the accusation that the content of its utopia is damaging to society, but it need not defend itself against the charge of being utopian.

The Right, as a conservative force, needs no utopia; its essence is the affirmation of existing conditions—a fact and not a utopia —or else the desire to revert to a state which was once an accomplished fact. The Right strives to idealize actual conditions, not to change them. What it needs is fraud, not utopia.

The Left cannot give up utopia because it is a real force even when it is merely a utopia. The sixteenth-century revolt of the German peasants, the Babouvist movement, and the Paris Commune were all utopian. As it turned out, without such utopian activities no nonutopian, progressive social changes would have taken place. Obviously, it does not follow that the task of the Left is to undertake extreme actions in every historical situation. All we are saying is that to condemn utopia for the mere fact that it is a utopia is rightist, conservative, and hampers the prospects of ever creating a utopia. In any event, we are not at the moment formulating social tasks. We are considering the concept of the Left completely in the abstract, trying to ascertain and not to postulate. Since the Left is as "normal" a social phenomenon as the Right, and progressive social movements are as normal as reactionary ones, it is equally normal for the Left, which is a minority, to be persecuted by the Right.

THE LEFT AND SOCIAL CLASSES

The concept of the Left remains unclear to this day. Although only about a hundred and fifty years old, it has acquired universal historical dimensions and is applied to ancient history by virtue of a diffusion of meaning common to all languages. Broadly used, the term has a practical function, but its meaning becomes very obscure, more sensed than understood. One thing is certain: It is easier to say which movements, programs, and attitudes are Left in relation to others than to determine where the Left ends and the Right begins in the political power relationship within society's total structure. We speak of a Left within Hitler's party, but that does not, of course, mean that the German Right was restricted to the party Right and that everything else, including the left wing of that party, was the Left in an absolute sense. Society cannot be divided into a Right and a Left. A leftist attitude toward one movement can be linked with a rightist attitude toward another. It is only in their relative meanings that these words make sense.

But what do we mean when we say a movement or an attitude is Left in relation to another? More specifically, which aspect of the concept of the Left is valid in all social situations? For example, what do we mean when we speak of the Left in the Radical Party of France, or of the social-democratic, Catholic, or communist Left? Is there some common element in the word used in such varied contexts? Or are we simply stating that every political situation reveals some human activity we either approve or find to be the less repugnant, and which we therefore call "the Left"? (I say "we call" because the Left draws the dividing line between the Left and the Right, while the Right fights this division systematically—and in vain, for the Left's self-definition is strong enough to define the Right and, in any event, to establish the existence of the demarcation line.)

No doubt because it has taken on a positive aura, the term "Left" is often appropriated by reactionary groups. For example, there is the "European Left," a political annex of the European Coal and Steel Community. So the mere use of the word does not define the Left. We must look for other signposts to help us fix our position in this murky area. Slogans like "freedom" and "equality" belong, of course, to the tradition of the Left; but they lost their meaning once they became universal catchwords to which everyone attaches his own arbitrary interpretation. As time passes, the Left must define itself ever more precisely. For the more it influences social consciousness, the more its slogans take on a positive aura, the more they are appropriated by the Right and lose their defined meaning. Nobody today opposes such concepts as "freedom" and "equality"; that is why they can become implements of fraud, suspect unless they are explained. What is worse, the word "socialism" has also acquired many meanings.

Naturally, it is quite easy to define the Left in general terms, as we can define "progress." But general definitions are necessarily misleading and difficult to apply in concrete discussions. For example, we can say that "Leftness" is the degree of participation in the process of social development that strives to eliminate all conditions in which the possibility of satisfying human needs is obstructed by social relations. From such a definition we derive a certain number of equally general slogans that are too universally acceptable to be useful in fixing political demarcations. The concepts of the Left, of progress, and of freedom are full of internal contradictions; political disputes do not arise from the mere acceptance or rejection of the concepts.

Therefore, rather than construct an easy though ineffective general concept of the Left applicable to all eras, let us accept existing social reality as a fact and look for the basic conflicts that define current history. These are, first of all, class conflicts and, secondarily, political ones. However, the political battle is not completely identical with the pattern of class relations; it is not a carbon copy of them transposed to relations between political parties. This is so because class divisions are not the only kind, and classes themselves are becoming more, rather than less, complicated because they are split from within by nationality or ideology. Finally, there are political divisions, in so far as they assume diverse forms of autonomy. Under these conditions political life cannot reflect class conflicts purely and directly but, on the contrary, ever more indirectly and confusedly. As a matter of fact, it was never otherwise—if it had been, all historical conflicts would have been resolved centuries ago. That is why the statement that it must be in the interest of the working class to belong to the Left does not always hold true. On the one hand, it is characteristic of the Left to try not to realize men's wishes against their will, nor to force them to accept benefits they do not desire. On the other hand, the working class of a given country may be greatly influenced by nationalism, yet the Left will not support nationalistic demands; elsewhere, the working class may have deep roots in a religious tradition, yet the Left is a secular movement. Even real immediate interests of the working class can be in opposition to the demands of the Left. For example, for a long time the English workers benefited from colonial exploitation—and yet the Left is an enemy of colonialism.

That is why the Left cannot be defined by saying it will always, in every case, support every demand of the working class, or that it is always on the side of the majority. The Left must define itself on the level of ideas, conceding that in many instances it will find itself in the minority. Even though in today's world there is no leftist attitude independent of the struggle for the rights of the working class, though no leftist position can be realized outside the class structure, and though only the struggle of the oppressed can make the Left a material force, nevertheless the Left must be defined in intellectual, and not class, terms. This presupposes that concrete intellectual life is not and cannot be an exact replica of class interests.

On this basis, we can set forth certain characteristics of the position of the Left in various social orders:

In capitalist countries the fight of the Left is to abolish all social privilege. In noncapitalist countries, it is to remove privileges that have grown out of noncapitalist conditions.

In capitalist countries the Left fights all forms of colonial oppression. In noncapitalist ones, it demands the abolition of inequalities, discrimination, and the exploitation of certain countries by others.

In capitalist countries the Left struggles against limitations on freedom of speech and expression. It does so also in noncapitalist lands. In one and the other the Left fights all the contradictions of freedom that arise in *both kinds* of social conditions: How far can one push the demand for tolerance without turning against the idea of tolerance itself? How can one guarantee that tolerance will not lead to the victory of forces that will strangle the principle of tolerance? This is the great problem of all leftist movements. It is also true, obviously, that the Left can make mistakes and act ineffectively, and thus engender a situation that is inimical to itself. However, it is not faulty tactics that are the distinguishing feature of the Left, for, as we have said, its criteria are established on an ideological plane.

In capitalist countries the Left strives to secularize social life. This is also true in noncapitalist countries.

In capitalist countries the destruction of all racism is an essential part of the Left's position. This is so in noncapitalist lands as well.

Everywhere the Left fights against the encroachment of any type of obscurantism in social life; it fights for the victory of rational thought, which is by no means a luxury reserved for the intellectuals, but an integral component of social progress in this century. Without it any form of progress becomes a parody of its own premises.

Finally, under both systems, the Left does not exclude the use of force when necessary, though the use of force is not an invention of the Left, but rather an unavoidable form of social existence. The Left accepts the antinomy of force, but only as an antinomy and not as a gift of fate. Everywhere the Left is ready to compromise with historical facts, but it rejects ideological compromises; that is, it does not abdicate the right to proclaim the basic tenets of its existence regardless of its political tactics.

The Left is free of sacred feelings; it has no sense of sanctity toward any existing historical situation. It takes a position of permanent revisionism toward reality, just as the Right assumes an attitude of opportunism in respect to the world as it is. The Right is the embodiment of the inertia of historical reality—that is why it is as eternal as the Left.

In both systems the Left strives to base its prospects on the experience and evolutionary tendencies of history; whereas the Right is the expression of capitulation to the situation of the moment. For this reason the Left can have a political ideology, while the Right has nothing but tactics.

Within the context of both systems, the Left knows that every human freedom satisfies a specific need, but that there is also a need for freedom as such.

The Left does not fear history. It believes in the flexibility of social relations and of human nature—in the possibility of changing them. Within both camps it rejects all humility vis-à-vis existing situations, authorities, doctrines, the majority, prejudgments, or material pressures.

In both, the Left—not excluding the use of force, not ashamed of it, and not calling it "upbringing" or "benevolence" or "care for children," etc.—nevertheless rejects any means of political warfare that lead to moral consequences which contradict its premises.

All this time I have been describing the Left as a certain ideological and moral attitude. For the Left is not a single, defined political movement, or party, or group of parties. The Left is a characteristic which to a greater or lesser degree can serve particular movements or parties, as well as given individuals or human activities, attitudes, and ideologies. One can be leftist from one point of view and not from another. There rarely occur political movements that are totally leftist in every aspect throughout the entire course of their existence. A man of the Left can participate in the political struggle and be a politician in a leftist party, but refuse to approve actions and opinions that are clearly inimical to a leftist attitude. Which does not mean, obviously, that the leftist position does not lead to internal conflicts and contradictions.

For these reasons the Left, as such and as a whole, cannot be an organized political movement. The Left is always to the left in certain respects with relation to some political movements. Every party has its left wing, a current which is farther to the left than the rest of the party in regard to some trait that can be cited as an example. Still, this does not mean that all the leftist elements of all parties taken together form a single movement, or that they are more closely allied to each other than they are to the party that gave birth to them. This would be so if they fulfilled all the requirements of being left in every aspect; but in that case they would not have been segments of so many diverse parties with such varied programs to begin with. The left wing of the Christian-democratic parties has, as a rule, infinitely more in common with them than with the socialist Left, yet it is the Christian-democratic Left on this very basis. Its "Leftness" may be shown by a stand on one or another actual political problem that, in the particular instance, brings it nearer the left of other parties—for example, a condemnation of colonialism or racism. On the other hand, the demands of the Left are met to varying degrees by different parties, which for this reason are called more or less leftist.

THE LEFT AND COMMUNISM IN POLAND

Can one speak of a pure party of the Left, and if so when? Is the Communist Party one? Since we cannot at this time define all the Communist parties, let us apply this question to the Polish Party.

For a long time the division into a Party Left and Right did not exist, although some members were more or less to the left. It did not exist because the Party was deprived of any real political life, because its ideology did not grow out of its own historical experience but was to a large degree imposed upon it regardless of experience. The division into a Left and a Right was drawn only when the political life of the Party came into being.

The split took place according to positions on the problems that always divide a movement into a Left and a Right. The Party Left was made up of those who fought to abolish all forms of privilege in social life, to recognize the principle of equality in dealings among nations, and to oppose local and foreign nationalism, reserving the right to call it by its real name of nationalism. The Left stands for the abolition, without chicanery, of all kinds of anti-Semitism in Poland, for freedom of speech and discussion, for *victory over dogma* and over dull, doctrinaire or else magical thinking in political life, for legality in public relations, for the maximum increase in the role of the working class within the system of government, for the liquidation of the lawlessness of the police. It fights against calling crimes "communism" and gangsters "communists"—and against a thousand other things.

I am listing these items summarily, without going into specifics, only to show that the direction of the changes intended to lead to the triumph of socialist democracy was inspired in the Party by its Left, whose demands on all vital points are included in what we call a leftist position. The Party Right consists of the forces of Stalinist inertia, defending a system based on principles that renounce Polish sovereignty in favor of a foreign nationalism. It supports the dictatorship of doctrinaire schemas in intellectual life, the dictatorship of the police in public life, and military dictatorship in economic life. It suppresses freedom of speech and uses the terminology of government by the people to conceal government by a political apparatus that disregards both the opinion of the public and its needs. The forces of Stalinism within the Party were and are a concentration of all the basic characteristics that define the Right, conservatism, and reaction.

However, the Left in the Polish Communist Party finds itself in a peculiar position, in which political tendencies do not cover a single unbroken gamut "from left to right," but abound in complications. The forces of the Left stand between two rightist tendencies: the reaction within the Party, and traditional reaction. This is a new historical development, awareness of which has arisen only in the past few years. It is as yet a very restricted phenomenon, but its implications are international. We will refrain from describing the historical causes of this situation, which in a certain phase of its development created a crisis in the communist movement, and simply state that the new Left appeared within the movement when it became apparent that a new Right existed. We will not at this time take up the question of just how the old Left degenerated and survived in the form of a Right—a process of which the history of Stalinism furnishes an instructive example—but it does not seem that this process was caused by the mere fact of the Left's coming to power. That is, it does not seem that the Left can exist only in a position of opposition, or that the possession of power is incompatible with the nature of the Left and leads inevitably to its downfall.

For although the negation of reality is part of the nature of the Left, it does not follow necessarily that reality must always be contrary to the demands of the Left. History, it is true, provides countless experiences that seem to speak for such a view and tempt us to see the Left as condemned to be an "eternal opposition." Yet over the years history has witnessed many setbacks to demands (for example, equality before the law) that subsequently, after centuries of suffering and defeat, became reality. Love of martyrdom and heroics is as alien to the Left as opportunism in a current situation or renunciation of utopian goals. The Left protests against the existing world, but it does not long for a void.

It is an explosive charge that disrupts the stability of social life, but it is not a movement toward nothingness.

THE WEAKNESSES OF THE LEFT

The main weakness of the Left was not that it grew out of negation, but that its negation attained only the level of moral protest and not of practical thought. A leftist attitude that stops at the stage of moral experience has little practical effect. "Bleeding-heartism" is not a political position.

Another trait, one that was unavoidable in our circumstances, was that the Left could not be an organized movement but only an unclear, fragmented negative consciousness opposed to the Right, which was bound by no scruples of loyalty regarding the formation of splinter factions within the Party. Thus the Left did not become a political movement in the true sense, but merely the sum total of spontaneous moral positions.

One weakness of the Left arose from the regressive circumstances of the international situation, the details of which I won't go into but which distinctly favored rightist activities.

Other weaknesses of the Left were those elements of the immediate situation from which the efforts of the Right could draw strength. The Right has no scruples about using every kind of demagogy, every political and ideological slogan that will enable it to dominate the situation of the moment. When necessary, it makes use of anti-Semitism to gain a certain number of allies from the bigots within or outside the party. The Right is primarily after power. In the fight for power (which, for example, it does not possess in Poland today) it is prepared to advance any leftist slogans that can count on popular appeal. Let us speak openly: Contempt for ideology is the strength of the Right because it allows for greater flexibility in practice and for the arbitrary use of any verbal façade that will facilitate the seizure of power. The Right is backed not only by the inertia of old customs and institutions, but also by the power of the lie; true, only a little way, but far enough to enable it to master the situation. At a given moment these ideological slogans are exposed as tactical imposture; but the trick is to make sure this moment comes only after the situation is in hand and the police are at one's disposal. That is why it is important for the Left to have available at all times criteria of recognition in the form of attitudes toward those actual political matters which, for one reason or another, force the Right to reveal itself for what it is. Today such criteria exist chiefly in the domain of international affairs.

The Left was also weakened by the fact that the general social protest against the compromised methods of the government was too often linked with reactionary demands unacceptable to the Left. But at that stage of its development, the Left was not strong enough to assume leadership of this protest.

As a result of these circumstances, the Left (on an international scale) could not help but be defeated. Nevertheless, if it is to exist, the Left must above all be aware of the danger of its *ideological* position.

The danger lies in its double exposure to two forms of rightist pressure. The Left must be particularly alert to its need to define its special position as *constantly and simultaneously* opposed to both those forces. It must clearly and continuously proclaim its negative stand against both rightist currents, of which one is the expression of Stalinist inertia and the other of the inertia of capitalism in its most backward and obscurantist cast. The Left is in grave danger if it directs its criticism toward only one pressure, for it thus blurs its political demarcations. Its position must be expressed in simultaneous negation. The Left must oppose Polish nationalism as adamantly as it does foreign nationalisms that threaten Poland. It must take the same clear rational attitude toward both the sclerotic religiosity of the Stalinist version of Marxism and the obscurantism of the clergy. It must simultaneously reject socialist phraseology as a façade for police states and democratic phraseology as a disguise for bourgeois rule. Only thus can the Left retain its separate, distinct position, which is that of a minority. Nevertheless, the Left does not desire to become a majority at any price.

In the current situation, the Left's greatest claim is ideological. To be more precise, it is to differentiate exactly between ideology and *current political tactics*. The Left does not refuse to compromise with reality as long as compromises are so labeled. It will always counteract any attempt to bend ideology to the demands of the moment, to temporarily necessary concessions, to tactics. While the Left realizes that on occasion it is powerless in the face of crime, it refuses to call crime a "blessing."

This is definitely not a trivial or secondary matter. A political party that does not rely on an authentic ideological base can exist for a long time in a state of vegetation, but it will collapse like a house of cards if confronted by difficulties. A case in point is the Hungarian Party. A communist movement that subordinates its ideology to immediate tactics is destined for degeneration and defeat. It can exist only with the support of the power and the repressive capacity of the state. The intellectual and moral values of communism are not luxurious ornaments of its activity, but the conditions of its existence. That is why it is difficult to create leftist socialism in a reactionary country. A communist movement whose sole form of existence is sheer tactics and which permits the loss of its original intellectual and moral premises ceases to be a leftist movement. Hence the word "socialism" has come to have more than one meaning, and is no longer synonymous with the word "Left." And this is why a regeneration of the concept of the Left is necessary—also so that we can delimit the meaning of socialist slogans. We therefore propose the term "leftist socialism."

Without surrendering any of the premises of its existence, the Left is obviously ready to make alliances with any groups, no matter how small, and with all "leftist foci" wherever they may be. But it must refuse to support rightist situations and activities; or if compelled to do so under duress, it must call this "duress" and refrain from seeking ideological justification for its actions.

The Left knows that these demands merely seem modest, and realizes they may lead to new defeats—but such defeats are more fruitful than capitulation. For this reason the Left is not afraid of being a minority, which is what it is on an international scale. It knows that history itself calls forth in every situation a leftist side which is as necessary a component of social life as its aspect of conservatism and inertia.

The contradictions of social life cannot be liquidated; this means that the history of man will exist as long as man himself. And the Left is the fermenting factor in even the most hardened mass of the historical present. Even though it is at times weak and invisible, it is nonetheless the dynamite of hope that blasts the dead load of ossified systems, institutions, customs, intellectual habits, and closed doctrines. The Left unites those dispersed and often hidden atoms whose movement is, in the last analysis, what we call progress.

Responsibility and History

The Escapist Conspiracy

The Opiate of the Demiurge

Conscience and Social Progress

History and Hope

The Escapist Conspiracy

Philosophy cannot produce its own subject matter.
We do a bad job of philosophizing on the basis of past
history if that history contains experiences which we
cannot repeat. We can pass reliable opinions only on
that which lies before us. . . . Men's actions ought not
so much be derived from their philosophy, as their
philosophy from their actions. Their history does not
stem from their way of thinking, but their way of
thinking—from their history.

Despite appearances, Karl Marx is not the author of these wise words; they were written more than half a century earlier by F. H. Jacobi, an author who for a variety of reasons may arouse a quite justifiable antipathy. Be that as it may, in this instance he formulated an extremely penetrating observation, worth bearing in mind whenever one undertakes any kind of philosophical or moral criticism.

In particular, it can constitute a useful subject for meditation when we set out to criticize any way of thinking distinguished by a systematic *abandonment* of *action*, political quietism, and ostentatious noninvolvement of the individual in the vexatious changes taking place in this world. Specifically, let us raise this question: What human actions can give birth to a philosophy that is the negation of action, if such a philosophy exists?

We pose this question not out of some abstract metaphysical consideration, but under the impact of current political experiences which have provided an unexpected opportunity to deliberate on the social commitment of the individual, the obstacles in the path of such commitment, and the philosophy that is to explain these obstacles or to justify morally man's impotence in the face of their inordinate resistance. What is more, these are matters that concern decent people who ask themselves how far they are willing to

87

become involved in not entirely decent situations, which actually constitute a major portion of their earthly existence.

A specific example of social noncommitment is the all-out escapist or "clerk,"[1] whose emergence in contemporary life represents—if we are to believe certain assurances—the main threat to the Polish state, the most venomous agent of disintegration still operating with impunity against the nation's united march toward a bright and glorious future. Poland is threatened by a vast network of sentimental escapists, by a shocking conspiracy of pale clerks poised on the stilts of lofty morals.

What is a clerk in the eyes of his adversary? A perfidious creature, full of deception, well aware that as long as he lives man cannot avoid participating in the conflicts of his time but who yet pretends that he can actually perform this miracle. Disguised as a guardian of universal human values, a costume lined with cowardice and hypocrisy, the clerk in reality longs to protect purely personal, private values that matter to no one but himself. This cosmic humbug would like to parade across the bloody swamps of history in the shining patent-leather slippers of private virtue. Failing this, he would rise above the mud of the times and waft his ethereal body on the wings of eternal values to the crystalline sphere of spiritual freedom, from which he could look down on the world with the eye of a pitiless judge. The clerk wishes to reserve to himself the right to moral judgment on social reality without assuming any responsibility. But only superficially, only in the minds of those he has managed to delude with his fantasies, does he avoid commitment to history.

In fact, he wades up to his neck in the sticky stuff, like everyone else, and acts on it with his slogans. He calls upon men to forsake action because decent people shouldn't become personally involved in the dirty business of settling historical accounts. Actually, refusal to act is in itself an action, though a purely negative one since it consciously abandons the field to the forces of social reaction. Since social nature abhors a vacuum, the holes made in it by the escapist are immediately filled by the brutal

---

1. As defined by Julien Benda in *La trahison des clercs.*—Trans.

aggression of reactionaries. This is how the clerk acts, knowing full well the consequences of his actions. He is, therefore, not ignorant but hypocritical, not a philosopher with clean hands but an active abettor of reaction.

And what is the anti-clerk in his own eyes? Someone who realizes fully that he must inevitably choose, willy-nilly, in the world's great conflicts. He commits himself consciously, not wishing to be engaged unwittingly and annexed against his will by one of the parties to the struggle. He knows, too, that in political contests, any third force is merely a sham, a fraud, and that an attack can be launched from only one position. The anti-clerk proclaims that he understands the moral aspect of political life, but he refuses to use an obsession with clean hands as a pretext to flee from the battlefield. So he cooperates with history to hasten its course, and not just to soothe his own conscience. He scorns the narcissism of moralists because their position is contrary to a morality based on the principle of responsibility. Since history acts brutally, he is prepared to accept its terms consciously, not out of personal pre-dilection but because it is impossible to reject them. He is, there-fore, a *realist*; he views the world from the vantage point of *existence*—as distinct from the clerk, who sees it in terms of what it ought to be, in terms of a fiction he himself has created and sought unsuccessfully to impose upon reality. In the confrontation, the escapist is, on contact with the real world, totally compromised by the defeat of his "ought."

Still, the matter is not all that simple. A dialogue with escapism has been going on for years in an impenetrable fog of adjectives —those parts of speech which are both most suggestive and most deceptive. We are dealing with a subject in which every attitude erects for itself an impressive verbal façade—proof that the dis-cussion seeks to avoid clear-cut, unequivocal questions, preferring rhetoric to argument.

Now what does an authentic clerk—in the "classical" sense as used by Benda—think of himself and his antagonist? The clerk feels that he has no intention whatsoever of subordinating his position to purely personal values. On the contrary, his chief concern is not to let himself be carried away by any group, class, or national interests, which inevitably conflict with values common to mankind as a whole and proper to man as such, to man as a member of a particular collectivity.

Man's decadence begins whenever that most human feature, rational understanding, becomes depraved in the service of national myths, emotions, and hatreds. An individual actively engaged in political conflicts can never attain the intellectual perspective that enables him to perceive the limitations of his own camp and the irrationality of undertakings in which he participates. Active struggle absorbs not only man's energy but also his mind, and narrows his scope to dimensions that reduce mankind to an animal level. What is most worthy in man, his ability to think rationally, can be safeguarded only by resolute resistance to all the temptations of relativism, by defending at all costs the fortress of imperishable values. If nobody preserves an objective and sober judgment in the midst of these great struggles, then mankind will exterminate itself more effectively than a cosmic disaster could.

CLERK: You are saying that at a given moment in history the specific interests of the working class become identical with the interests of mankind as a whole, that they not only retain all human values but are alone capable of salvaging them. Yet what evidence can you offer in support of this view except vague historical-philosophical speculation? Why should I abandon, on the spot, the noblest values of human existence in the name of this speculative dialectic of the future?

Our experience so far does not justify such optimism. On the contrary, it teaches us that those specific interests, as you understand them, have frequently been realized in opposition to universal human values. There are examples: one, two, thousands! Though you may represent a given historical reality, by what right do you demand that I approve it morally merely because it is a reality? I refuse to support any form of historical existence on the basis of its inevitability—for which I see no evidence at this time.

If crime is the law of history, is that sufficient reason for me to become a criminal myself? Why? You won't allow me to measure your moves against the yardstick of absolute values because in your opinion these are sheer fabrication. Yet on the other hand, you speak of universal human values that are presumably, by the same token, absolute. You therefore quietly introduce absolute axioms into your doctrine, though in a vague and equivocal form, only to destroy them immediately with an equally ambiguous historical relativism.

You come to me with this baggage and expect me to renounce all the best that civilization has created because your eschatology promises to return it intact after some unspecified lapse of time. You demand unlimited moral credit for your historiosophy and your history, although both reveal their bankruptcy at every step. It is not you who stand for the philosophy of responsibility—you who recklessly agree to sacrifice everything to the Moloch of immediate reality in the unsubstantiated hope that all will be restored. He who is really willing to shoulder responsibility for the treasures history has discovered and produced will defend them at any cost, even at the price of disengaging himself from current struggles, if the only way to preserve these values lies outside the field of battle.

ANTI-CLERK: It is, nevertheless, worth noting that you can save these values only by saving your own skin. Also, it is peculiar that while you cast doubt on my historical arguments, you fail to see what direction the other side of history is taking. There is no longer room for doubt. Over there, books are burned on pyres. What have you done to save them? Do you think it is enough for you to learn them by heart? Over there, people's guts are ripped out and their faces trampled on by hobnailed boots. What did you do to prevent it? Do you think preaching to armed soldiers about universal love will do any good? Or do you believe you'll extinguish those fires by repeating the Ten Commandments?

CLERK: Pyres burn on both sides of Mount Sinai. Will counting them give you a feeling of moral superiority? That would be a cheap victory. You persist in telling me that the threat to human freedom is so great that in order to combat it one must renounce liberty. You keep harping on Saint-Just's slogan: "No freedom for the enemies of freedom." I am willing to agree up to a point; but I must know who determines the friends and foes of freedom. It is always someone committed to one of the camps. This is like a trial in which one person is simultaneously plaintiff, judge, prosecutor, and policeman.

My involvement, which is constantly forced down my throat, must be based on an absolute faith in this man and his present and future intentions. In other words, I must place more confidence in him than I am willing to accord myself. Why should I prevail upon myself to place such complete trust in a man who insists on acting as the court even while he is a party to the proceedings? That is to deny the eternal and most elementary principle of justice. He will not allow the conflict between him and his adversary to be settled by anyone but himself. Yet in order to render a just verdict a judge must be impartial, unbiased, when he takes over his duties—that is to say, he discharges his functions properly only when he applies the same criteria of abstract justice to both parties to the dispute. Yet you refuse me this right, claiming that I must first be on your side before I can form a just opinion, that I have the right to be a judge only when I am one of the contenders.

To vindicate this shocking rule you have, it is true, a theory all your own, that no third force can exist in a society torn by class antagonisms. This theory renders the role of judge, as conceived by modern jurisprudence, altogether impossible. You regard this theory as self-evident and demand that I accept it. If I reject it and desire to act as a judge in the dispute, you automatically place me in your opponents' camp. Because I recognize the possibility of a third force, I am immediately classified an antagonist and as such deprived of the moral right to assess the merits of your case —for then I am part of the controversy. I can avoid this only if I accept your theory of the nonexistence of a third force and espouse your point of view: I can judge and understand you only if I am one of you. Don't you see you're arguing just like Søren Kierkegaard, who said that in order to understand Christianity one had to believe in it?

You are saying the same thing: to appreciate you, one must first accept your reasoning. Surely you are aware that this demand is unacceptable to any rational being in the world; rationalism means, among other things, abstaining from making a choice until all the arguments are weighed. But your postulate bids me accept your thinking before I am given the right to examine it. The entire experience of European culture warns me against this manifestation of total irrationality. I do not deny that your method may win you many adherents, but please note that you cannot win them by intellectual means. Your position is completely 'impermeable'; it cannot be penetrated by rational thinking for it repels *a priori* all criticism as an intrinsically hostile act necessarily launched—consciously or unconsciously—from the opposing camp. Sensible human beings will find your theory of the nonexistence of a third force fundamentally irrational and indigestible.

And if you continue to argue that I protect myself together with those unalterable cultural values you scoff at, and if on those grounds you wish to show me up as an escapist enamored of himself, then my answer is that I've no intention of becoming a scoundrel merely to demonstrate that I do not care whether or not I have the reputation of being an honest man.

ANTI-CLERK: Your defense is your indictment.

CLERK: I am not defending myself. Why do you always divide the world into prosecutors and defendants?

ANTI-CLERK: I didn't invent this world. One must face its horrors without wailing. You accuse us revolutionaries of splitting the world in two and of insisting that people commit themselves to only one side. There is as much point in this as there is in upbraiding meteorologists for hail and tornadoes. The entire history of mankind supports our argument. Another proof is the actual effectiveness of our social action, which is based precisely on this interpretation of conditions.

CLERK: History proves everything the historian chooses to deposit in it beforehand. You analyze history on the basis of a ready-made diagram and then announce triumphantly that this same diagram emerged from your analysis, forgetting to add that you put it there in the first place. And the practical efficacy of this interpretation has not been proven. The extent to which a given movement is truly effective historically can be measured only when its time is over, after the event. By claiming that for the first time in history you are free of the limitations a man's era imposes on his outlook, you fall prey to the same mystification you rightly discern in your predecessors.

ANTI-CLERK: *In qua mensura mensi fueritis, remetietur vobis.* (As you mete out unto others, so it shall be measured unto you.) You are saying that we are drunk with our alleged freedom from historical limitations, while you are truly free, since you pretend to rule over a world of eternal values that transcend history and are not subject to its pressures. We, on the contrary, recognize clearly the relativity of values and, what is more, we are the only ones who have acquired the ability to think historically, and this enables us to observe the present in its continuous flow.

CLERK: Yes, you *proclaim* the general principle of historicism, but I cannot see that you practice it. I would not reproach you for this or even for your inconsistency if you accepted what I propose as an alternative possibility—namely, the recognition of values that cannot be canceled under any conditions and whose negation is evil regardless of circumstances. But you act differently. Your relativism hides behind a mask of fictitious immutability. Your values change fundamentally every day, and daily they are pronounced final. This is the worst form of relativism, because it inters historical thinking (whose worth I do not deny) as well as the unalterable and lasting achievements of mankind. It is a peculiar cult that professes monotheism but changes its god daily.

Our is a strange discussion. It rather closely parallels Romain Rolland's fictional dialogue between Carnot and Lavoisier. A certain naïveté in that drama does not conceal the analogy. Carnot demands that the other sacrifice the present for the sake of the future. Lavoisier replies that to sacrifice the truth, self-respect, and all other human values to the future is tantamount to sacrificing the future. I cannot disagree with him. Since I do not share your faith, as optimistic as it is unsubstantiated, regarding the predictability of things to come, I never know what effects our present actions will have in the future. Therefore I cannot agree with the idea of offering up great moral and cognitive values on the altar of uncertain future objectives. However, I do know that the means used necessarily imprint their stigma on the final results.

ANTI-CLERK: You have been duped by the mendacious picture that liberal politicians always paint of the revolutionary movement so as to make it loathsome. We are not engaged in constructing an eschatology that devours the present. In fact, the present benefits from the revolution; and thanks to this, it is possible to renounce some potentials for the sake of a better future instead of exploiting them fully now. All the measures that shock you so are in every instance a defense against a greater evil. Remember that in politics a choice between two evils is far more common than a choice between absolute good and evil. And that is a premise of reality that neither one of us created.

CLERK: I will never believe that the moral and intellectual life of mankind follows the laws of economic investments: expecting a better tomorrow because of saving today, lying so that truth may triumph, taking advantage of crime to save nobility. I know that sometimes we have to choose between two evils. But when both possibilities are extremely evil, I will do my utmost to refrain from making a choice. In this way I do choose, be it only man's right to make his own evaluation of the situation in which he finds himself. This is no small matter.

ANTI-CLERK: Nevertheless, reverting to your example, history proved Carnot right.

CLERK: I hadn't noticed.

ANTI-CLERK: In that case, to continue our conversation we must re-interpret the whole history of the world—an impossible task, especially if we have to wait until it is done before we make a choice that must be made at once.

CLERK: You have something there. Since we are forced to take a stand on current changes, we obviously cannot wait upon the uncertain outcome of historiosophical discussions, which can remain nebulous for a hundred years. This being so, our choice is always best if it is determined by that particle of certainty we do possess. Lasting moral values, continuously evolving up to now, are the surest support available if reality demands that we make a choice, which, after all, is also of a moral nature. In any case, they are more trustworthy than any historiosophy. And that, ultimately, is why I will stick to my opinion.

ANTI-CLERK: Whatever happens?

CLERK: Whatever happens.

This dialogue has been going on for decades. We leave it undecided because we do not wish to take part in it. It is not only unresolved but unresolvable. Moreover, it occurs in a sphere where bullets never hit the target but go off on tangents, because the common assumptions indispensable to a meaningful discussion do not exist. We should like to transpose the discussion to a level where the arguments on both sides can be partially accepted. The opposition between the two viewpoints will not thus be eliminated, but the polarities themselves will undergo a change.

To do this, we must first see the clerk from the outside, as a product of the situation in which he finds himself. The clerk imagines he has made himself independent of history by clinging to things eternal; in reality, he has been pushed into this position. He is a humanist burdened with all the traditions of humanism, which he does not want to discard. And this, he believes, is precisely what he would have to do if he were to join either of the big camps whose battles determine the history of the world. He voluntarily dissociates himself from history and renounces social action because it requires him to pass through the customs house of political realism where he would be stripped of all those values so precious to him.

When we begin to condemn escapism, that is a sign that social conditions favoring its spread have come about. Whenever a given moral norm, whether negative or positive, comes alive in the consciousness of society, it proves that conditions exist which require that this norm be broken, for it serves as a barrier against some real tendency in society. If the commandment "Do not steal" assumes a vital importance in society, this means that society has given rise to the need to steal on a large scale. When clerks are attacked, it is obvious that escapism has found a good breeding ground. To say that clerks are contemptible petits bourgeois may express an indomitable fighter's scorn for escapism, but it does not explain what social situations favor the proliferation of escapist attitudes. It is wrong to hold that these are situations in which revolutions are either impending or taking place, for revolutions least favor escapism. On the contrary, everything seems to indicate they are post-revolutionary—that is, when revolution is least likely but when, at the same time, the polarization of political forces is greatest and the political choices are reduced to two, each unacceptable for various reasons. Clerkism is the defeat of political choice, a flight from commitment that rationalizes itself as a defense of suprahistorical values when in actual fact it shows the impossibility of finding values in current history.

The problem of a single alternative is one of the most important of our time. It most adequately expresses the experience of the Stalinist era and the main tendency of the political Left resulting from that experience. The whole complex of recent political and intellectual attempts at the ideological renaissance of the revolutionary Left—attempts whose effects and effectiveness cannot be foreseen at present—may be characterized generally as an attempt to break through the traditional Stalinist *blackmail of a single alternative* in political life. The permanent Stalinist line was, in fact, to try to create situations where every criticism of Stalinism would amount, objectively, to an automatic adherence to the reactionary camp, to an automatic declaration of solidarity with capitalist imperialism. Stalinism forestalled all social criticism by labeling it counterrevolutionary. That is why its most furious and brutal attacks were always leveled against the forces farthest to the left and closest to the ideals of communism. No one was more oppressed and persecuted, no one was the object of more deadly hatred or greater police brutality than the independent left wing—communist or communizing movements that were critical of Stalinist practice and doctrine. The social-democratic Right was at least dealt with in political terms, whereas Trotskyism and Titoism were fought as foreign espionage. Although the press was occasionally permitted to publish speeches by bourgeois politicians, mention of the activities of the non-Stalinist Left was unthinkable. It would be naïve to find this practice surprising; it is both understandable and explicable. After all, for centuries the stake was reserved for heretics and not heathens; and very rarely do books by non-Catholics appear on the Church's index.

That special, pitiless hatred which almost every organization with a political ideology harbors for its heretics, dissidents, apostates, or renegades is a familiar phenomenon. It is a hundred times more violent than the revulsion felt for undisputed and recognized enemies. As a matter of fact, this hatred is an understandable—though not exclusive—by-product of all social conditions in which a given political or religious organization *becomes an end in itself,* even though its originators regarded it only as a means to an end. We say "not exclusive," bearing in mind the fact that the chief threat to every militant group, particularly if it is a minority, is those elements of internal subversion that sap its coherence and fighting capacity from within. External pressure is, within limits, a stimulus for the consolidation of the group, but internal hotbeds of dissent always bode death.

However, the phenomenon we are describing cannot be explained simply as the natural self-defense of a political organism against an invasion of foreign bodies. It is not immunization against disease-bearing germs, but an attempt to develop an epidermis invulnerable to stimuli likely to produce evolutionary changes—a symptom of regression in the social process.

Unflagging vigilance over its own meticulous boundary lines is an essential characteristic of every social group that can be called a "sect"—constant control to assure precise and unambiguous criteria differentiating it from the entire outside world. These criteria are of various sorts: ideological, organizational, traditional, ritualistic; and the greater their number, pettiness, and variety, the more advanced the ossification of the sect. When this condition prevails, it becomes apparent that the social organism, to an ever increasing extent, no longer sustains itself by natural assimilation and communication with its environment, but somehow, miraculously, through an unnatural process of reproduction, feeds on its own substance. Its activities are self-centered, and its external acts are determined by its need for self-preservation. The sect must take infinite care lest somewhere on its fringes the boundary dividing it from its environment become blurred. It is a creature incapable of natural procreation; thus self-preservation is its only reason for being. While it can increase its weight, it can neither develop nor conceive. Since creation is organically impossible within its scope, prolongation of its individual existence becomes its exclusive pursuit. Every act of creation means, of necessity, going outside the sect, and therefore breaking through its frontiers.

The phenomenon of sectarianism in political life, manifesting itself among other things in this scrupulousness over the precise boundaries of the organization, is proof of a twofold process taking place within the group: its progressive senility, and its loss of the power of reproduction. The political organism has become an end in itself, alienated from the social tasks that created it and interested only in the self-imposed goal of prolonging its own existence. Sectarianism is not an error of individuals; it is a social portent of death. Under these circumstances, political suspiciousness, on the surface absurd and pathological, becomes an understandable social (not individual) phenomenon. It is comparable to that brutal egoism which occasionally accompanies old age, when one dimly feels that nature is turning against one; it is a convulsive self-defense of a social form of existence that history has turned against. When the police become the sole arbiter of social life, they act as a surgical scalpel performing a cruel operation on an organism that has lost its capacity for natural resistance: they become an artificial reaction to the signs of doom and express the mentality of a creature that cannot count on pity—for pity is known only to human beings, not to nature or to history.

I hope scientists will forgive the biological inadequacy of my metaphor. It is merely an attempt to symbolize one of the characteristics of a political phenomenon called, more or less exactly, Stalinism. Regardless of its dimensions, Stalinism is a sect. A party of the Stalinist type no longer regards itself as a means to an end, but rather as an end in itself and thus autonomous of the social forces that engendered it. The emergence within it of a single organized sector—the party apparatus which dominates the whole—is the external manifestation of this process. When that apparatus becomes the only driving force in the life of the party, the existence of special interests of the apparatus bears witness to the special interests of the party. What Stalinism implies in the life of Communist parties is not that they are so badly organized that they do not allow for the control of the party masses over the authorities; it means that the *social function of the party* is to render impossible a change in this type of organization.

As a political movement, Stalinism surrounded itself with an impenetrable ideological and ritualistic fence, defining both itself and all remaining social reality in terms of itself. There are no connecting passages, no intermediate stages leading to the rest of the world from the strict and arbitrary frontiers that Stalinism has drawn. Stalinism stubbornly regards all other existing boundaries as trifling and unessential. The only socially significant division is the line that delineates Stalinism as a camp. The world is split into those who are saved and those who are condemned, into the kingdom of God and the realm of Satan, the line between them clearer than that separating a mountain from a valley. This frontier passes through every phase of life: every fact, every thought, every particle that constitutes the material of society is eternally stamped by its adherence to one or the other of these realms. The tribe of Abel and the tribe of Cain divide between themselves all ideas, tools, social relations, morality, art, science, tradition, and, further, private feelings and predilections —nature itself, almost. No neutral or mixed areas exist between these two kingdoms; integral annexation to one or the other is the only possibility.

That is why Stalinism exacted either total acceptance or total rejection; and it was remarkably successful in imposing this scheme on the rest of the world. Every new ritual and every new truth had to be accepted under threat of irrevocable banishment from the company of the blessed. To question the priority of Yablochkov[2] over Edison was tantamount to questioning the dictatorship of the proletariat. We stress the fact that the connection between these two assertions was not imaginary, *it was real.* No effort was spared to make it real, to make it a social fact. Stalinism peopled its world with a thousand new deities, each demanding worship under threat of excommunication on grounds of atheism. There was really no difference between disbelief in the miracles of St. Expeditus and outright godlessness. Partisanship permeated every aspect of the world, so much so that sometimes even the forces of nature seemed to be part of it: for many years the Stalinist press made natural disasters appear to be the monopoly of capitalist countries and proof of a failure of their system.

We invoke this picture not to ridicule—it is easy to caricature certain features—but to depict that essential quality of the Stalinist era, the imposition of a single alternative on human reality in all spheres of social life. This pattern was not merely officialdom's myth, it functioned in fact. Stalinism did define its enemies

---

2. A Soviet physicist.—TRANS.

by defining itself. Its mechanism served to promote the permanent consolidation of its enemies, for it cast on them a uniformly
dark shadow which blurred all differences. This is, among other
things, the cause of the Stalinist party's organic inability to rally
allies and its chronic incapacity to set up a Popular Front. For a
Popular Front can be effectively conceived only in terms of a
compromise, of divergence of opinion and action in certain
fields and agreement in others recognized as essential at a given
moment. In the Stalinist interpretation, however, the Popular
Front must be based not on compromise, but exclusively on
total hegemony. Only those were admitted who accepted the
assumptions of Stalinism in essential matters and who at least
had no opinions on other issues.

The one concession a Stalinist party accords its allies is the
right not to speak their minds on certain secondary matters; it
does not give them the right to voice a conflicting view on any
issue at all. For example, an alliance with anticolonial forces
against colonialism is impossible if they do not forbear to express
themselves regarding the Moscow trials. At best the ally has the
right to keep silent on certain subjects; he may then merit being
called an immature and inconsistent ally, but still an ally. Yet
woe betide him if he raises a critical voice on any question whatsoever: he will be cast summarily into the enemy camp. Questioning the legality of the Bukharin trial is identical with the desire
to set up a police state on the blood spilled by workers and peasants.

Despite what one might think, this interpretation of the world
in terms of one alternative was a tremendous asset to the Stalinist system. On the face of it one would suppose that the systematic extermination of potential allies, the demand that one's
views be accepted totally and absolutely, would be the best
method of committing suicide. In reality, however, this depends
on the purpose of the organization. An aging sect can ill afford
allies, for it is dominated by an urge to survive, which thrusts
upon it an obsessive fear that it may lose its boundaries. The more
the sect becomes an end in itself, the more its efforts are concen-
trated on perpetuating its own survival and eking out its vitality,
the more keenly it is bound to feel every criticism, even the

most minor, as a menace to the very foundations of its existence. The whole external world becomes an enemy, not because of one individual's idiosyncrasies, but because of the objective situation. Everyone who is "different" is a foe, for the sect, having forfeited its capacity for progressive evolution, can only hold all changes to be threats of disintegration.

Needless to say, Stalinism stocked in its arsenal the slogan of unity, voiced in a tone of constant indignation. Stalinist thought was idealistic in nature and the constant reiteration of slogans was necessary for many reasons; but when it became evident that they did not make unity any less fictitious or remote, Stalinist ideologists could do nothing but bewail man's gross ingratitude and accuse the other contracting parties of bad faith. "We do everything to bring about the unity of the labor movement: we repeat the slogan of unity. Yet we fail. Hence it is obvious that the other side is hardened in its hatred of progress." That is how the Stalinist ideologist sees the world. He is unable to examine the social circumstances of which he himself is an element and as a result of which the real unity of the workers' movement is an unattainable ideal. Consequently he is bound to seek the explanation in the sphere of pure spirit—in the spitefulness of his adversaries, in their ill will and ignorance, or, best of all, in their deceptive intentions and subversive plans. Such an attitude is natural to the Stalinist ideologist, who cannot admit the idea that he might ever be rightly criticized on any issue whatsoever or that he could ever revise any of his assumptions, for they are sacred. In his mind, unity can present itself only as a voluntary renunciation on the part of his allies of all principles irreconcilable with Stalinism. And since his mind is conditioned to exclude a priori even a shadow of criticism, he is genuinely indignant and astonished at the failure of his appeals.

In the seventeenth century the problem of the unity of Christendom was very much a live issue in various religious movements. The champions of that goal, gathered together in what has come to be called the Irenic Movement, dreamed of a fantastic utopia. They hoped to establish which dogmas were common to all Christianity and to forge them into a universal faith which, though perhaps poor in substance, would be morally effective and would end religious wars and the cleavages in the Christian world. This idea, associated with the concepts of Herbert of Cherbury, had many followers. It was propagated by Dutch Anabaptists and Socinians; many outstanding French freethinkers were among its protagonists; Leibnitz was one of its most zealous adherents. It prospered in certain ruling houses—it was discussed at the court of the Prussian king. In some places, temples common to all Christian religions were built. Even King Ladislas IV was deeply interested in the question of uniting the churches. Frequent attempts were made to formulate the common content of Christianity that could be the basis for this unity.

The great Bossuet spoke up on behalf of the Roman Catholic Church, explaining that he, of course, supported the idea of unification; to achieve it, the Protestants should admit their errors, convert to the true faith, and recognize the authority of the Pope. He made it clear that the Roman Catholic Church would not, obviously, relinquish any element of its doctrine. This stand was by no means cynical; indeed, it is entirely understandable. If Bossuet had been asked why he refused to renounce any part of the dogma, even for the sake of unity, he would have replied, "But this doctrine alone, and no other, is true. To abandon any of its tenets is to betray truth." The Church strives for unity with the Protestants and is ready for it at any time, provided they convert to the Roman faith.

We have no reason to blame this way of thinking on the energetic bishop's stupidity: it was not his individual thinking, nor in fact was it thinking at all. It was the natural reaction of a political organization to proposals that were bound to lead to a loss of its individuality. Naturally, the chief object of the Roman Catholic Church is to preserve that individuality. As a political entity, it has its own special interests and naturally has no intention of committing suicide for the sake of religious unity or world peace.

Clearly, every political organization for which self-preservation is an end in itself must follow the same pattern. It can conceive of unity only as a conversion of its partners. A Stalinist party can no more have allies than the Roman Church can rally around it "allied" sects whose dogma "slightly" differs from its own. For example, one of them would not recognize, let us say, transubstantiation; a second would reject resurrection; a third, the concept of the Trinity. Try asking a Catholic bishop to overlook these "slight" discrepancies and to recognize a common doctrinal platform on the remaining issues as a basis for unity! It is obvious that to a faithful Catholic the difference between an Anabaptist and an atheist is virtually insignificant as compared to the gulf that separates them both from orthodoxy. There is no salvation outside the Church. The world is not divided into a multiplicity of views that form a continuum from orthodox Catholicism to atheism; it is split between the Catholics and all the others. A dualistic, truly Manichaean vision of reality is an inevitable form of sectarian thinking. To condemn it morally is senseless. *Naturalia non sunt turpia.*

Only the material strength of the sect, then, determines to what degree this picture of the world will correspond to reality. Stalinism was a powerful sect, and the genius of hypocrisy was on its side. It created a reality whose fundamental divisions approximated its mental image—a reality in which any criticism of Stalinism really had to be phrased very carefully lest it turn into an apologia of capitalism, a situation toward which it was systematically pushed. The forces of social reaction were strong, the forces of the independent Left, weak. Because of the absence of a major social focus that would retain their criticism within the orbit of socialist thought, dissidents from Stalinist communism were easily transformed into renegades. Apostasy is not at all an imaginary phenomenon; those ex-revolutionaries who in fact—and not only in the opinion of their former comrades—defect to the Right are renegades, even though everything may have been done to facilitate the change. Doriot[3] was a renegade. Arthur Koestler is a renegade, not because he wrote *Darkness at Noon* —which has become a part of contemporary culture—but because

---

3. Jacques Doriot, a French Communist who became a leader of the fascist Croix de Feu during the period before the Second World War.— TRANS.

of his activities in the past few years. Pierre Hevré is well on the way to becoming a renegade, not because he published *Révolution et les fétiches*, a timid and weak criticism of some Stalinist tenets, but because he subsequently displayed a readiness to align himself with authentic reaction as the lesser of two evils compared with Stalinism. The fact that he was pushed onto this road is beside the point. It merely illustrates the aforementioned effectiveness of Stalinist political practices.

Renegades are all those surprisingly numerous people who, after breaking with communism, see in it the sole threat to the world and in the fight against it are ready to ally themselves with anyone—colonialists, active counterrevolutionaries, and the extreme Right. Obsessed with their anticommunist mission, they begin to see fascism as a specter invented by the Stalinists, and anti-Stalinism becomes a sufficient basis for an understanding with every former opponent. They tacitly accepted Stalin's version of reality, namely the nonexistence of a third force, and themselves illustrate its validity. Blackmailed into accepting the idea that only one alternative exists, when they leave one camp they voluntarily relocate in the other. Renegades are one of the great triumphs of Stalinism; they are constant proof of its rightness. The transformation of dissidents into renegades, of which there are thousands of examples, is actually an effect of that system. Stalinism's efficacy manifested itself in the fact that it had no allies, and the fact that the forces of the Left which refused to be swallowed up whole or pushed behind counterrevolutionary barricades were numerically so weak and had such difficulty in remaining alive.

Stalinism—by taking advantage of this situation, by sanctioning it metaphysically with its theory of two forces and the inevitable polarization of social life between them, by paralyzing criticism as an automatic adherence to the reactionary camp—imposed on the mind of the Left a fateful choice between heaven and hell. Whoever thought it was a choice between two kinds of hell was judged not as an opponent of both but as a supporter of the enemy.

There is no greater danger to the development of the socialist movement in its present phase than to permit a renewed intensification of the political polarization that tends toward a single alternative. This assumption is the starting point for all efforts to give substance to the concept of "political realism" in current politics. Whatever the factors leading to the disappearance of criticism within the bounds of socialism, the result would be to force legitimate criticism into the position of the counterrevolution, where it could be taken over by obscurantist, clerical social forces aiming to restore capitalism. In that event, escapism would offer the only alternative to a choice between being a renegade or a loyal opportunist. Yet to choose escapism means resigning from active participation in political life and capitulating in the face of existing choices. The violence of the attack on the clerk is proportionate to the degree of this political polarization. As we have pointed out, the attempt to break through this alternative nature of political existence epitomizes the trend toward a renaissance of the long-compromised revolutionary movement. To destroy that trend would be tantamount to liquidating all the forces, no matter how weak, that are capable of preventing democratic criticism from being classified as counterrevolutionary; capable of forestalling a situation where the economic demands of the working class are considered sabotage, where every voice of political criticism speaks for solidarity with Western imperialism, where every discussion of the limits of social liberties is the work of clerical elements, and every economic criticism the triumph of shopkeepers and speculators.

Socialist criticism is indispensable for an effective opposition to real counterrevolutionary criticism. The absence of a possibility of it is unavoidably indentifiable with a growth of administrative and repressive methods of ruling, a development that is then inevitable because it derives not from anyone's intentions but from the course of political life. Moreover, this is the reverse of the building of socialism. Unfavorable economic conditions increase the danger because they deepen the gulf between working-class demands and the resources of the state as employer. This is expressed in intensified conflicts between the mind of the masses and the political organization of the state and its representatives.

As we well know, the lure of capitalism is very great in Poland. This social amnesia—deplorable, but practically incurable—does not present capitalism as it existed in pre-1939 Poland: crippled, technically backward, obscurantist and clerical in culture, fascist in politics. Today capitalism appears as the high standard of living in West Germany, Great Britain's political democracy, the technology of the United States. To say that British democracy is feasible only if you have centuries of England's history behind you is one hundred per cent correct, but it is just as indubitable that it is practically impossible to instill this truth in the mind of the public. It is almost as hard to convince the mass of the people that one cannot transfer Poland to the British Isles as it would be to carry out that shift in reality.

To try to overcome capitalism's attractiveness with historical information is a pipe dream. Its attraction does not stem from ignorance of past history but from events taking place now. Capitalism as it exists in fact and is actually visible can be resisted effectively only by the attractiveness of a really existing and actually visible socialism. If Poland crushed capitalism in a country lagging in its development and ruined by the war, the socialist movement in this land bears not only the weight of having to catch up with the technical level of the capitalist world, but also the equally heavy burden of breaking down the persistent and inevitable inertia in the mind of society regarding capitalism. The antinomy of the Polish social pattern consists, among other things, in the fact that this inertia cannot be overcome by direct methods, but only indirectly, by making daily life socialist and attractive at the same time. Yet this very inertia makes the latter task difficult. So these difficulties stimulate each other.

Apart from economic changes, which are felt directly by the working population, the difficulties can be counteracted either by the force of repression or by the power of socialist consciousness. The latter is, to a large extent, in direct proportion to the extent of *permissible* socialist criticism, and that, in turn, is inversely proportionate to *actual* counterrevolutionary criticism.

Thus the resources of social reaction grow as effective possibilities of socialist and democratic criticism diminish. In the same way, the need—not simply the intention—to resort to repression increases, and so does the role it must perform in the system of government. For this reason, the pressure that seeks to paralyze socialist criticism must entail repressive measures against the masses, for it causes all criticism to become a tool of political reaction.

History seems to teach that comedies of national unity last only a few weeks in the life of one generation, whereas tragedies of national controversies fill the rest of its time. Poland's most important social task is to assure that the greatest number of these conflicts are played out on the stage set by socialism. This must also be the positive program of socialist criticism, which from conviction wishes to be both critical and socialist, but which is tempted to abstain from speaking when necessity confronts it with a choice between apostasy and opportunism. That abstention is precisely the position of the clerk—explicable, though not morally justifiable, by the objective conditions of the political world. Escapism is capitulation. However, we are concerned not with stating this truth but with investigating the reality within which the idea of capitulation can grow into a social force. Contemporary escapism as the ideology of renouncing choice results from the confrontation of two social facts: the ideological consciousness of the anti-Stalinist left on the one hand, and a reality that bars this consciousness from asserting itself in social life on the other.

Escapism cannot be disarmed by the mere slogan of "political realism." For what does that slogan mean? Lacking more precise commentary, it loses all factual content and becomes a mere military watchword, one of a thousand ideological missiles hurled by political polemicists to gain a tactical advantage. In daily political practice, the concept of "realism" sheds not a flicker of light on reality; it is solely invective aimed at an opponent. Spokesmen for "realism" want to convince the public that they use this term to mean that they "take reality into account," don't go off on wild goose chases, don't build castles in the air, don't bite off more than they can chew, and the like. In other words, they try to persuade themselves and others that everything they proclaim in their political program can easily be deduced from the trivial principle of taking facts into account. Their adversaries, on the other hand, builders of imaginary utopias, despise reality and believe it can be molded to their visions. They are visionaries with rampant imaginations, and as such, social mischief-makers and manufacturers of myths.

In reality things are not that simple. If these alleged utopians were indeed a handful of visionaries conjuring up pictures of a perfect world out of their own minds, nobody would bother to attack them. But when criticism of a utopian doctrine becomes a major social preoccupation, this means that such a doctrine is a serious factor in the social consciousness and plays an important part in the social situation in which the advocate of "realism" wants to do his work. Therefore this sort of campaign against utopianism does not in any way resemble Engels' critique of Fourier. For it is a criticism not of utopia's social inefficiency but precisely of its efficacy, an efficacy that, in the opinion of its critics, is undesirable and harmful because it hampers the political efforts that the situation demands.

The dispute over the watchword "political realism" is intellectually barren and degenerates into a show of naked slogans so long as it is not a concrete debate about the real *limits of applicability* of that concept, whose general usefulness no one questions. That is, this must be a discussion of which specific claims are realistic and which are utopian, and in what sense. Otherwise we sink to a recitation of general phrases about realism which are suitable for universal consumption but only camouflage existing differences. Let us remember, generalities can justify absolutely everything.[4]

---

4. Ten or eleven years ago, a vast debate was waged in Poland on the subject of socialist humanism and the relationship between ethics and history. The arguments advanced against escapism, utopianism, and naïve sermonizing as substitutes for historical analysis are revived today in unaltered form, just as if a cycle of history had been completed and we had to return to our starting point. In those days, this writer in his polemical en-

We shall not, at present, go into the question of the concrete limits of the applicability of the concept of political realism, and we shall leave things at a refusal to discuss whether or not reality should be taken into account. For the issue thus presented is spurious. Whenever a critic replies that "the laws of nature cannot be broken," instead of proving that the specific proposition is contrary to some definite and tested law of nature, we know we are talking to someone who is indifferent to argument and reason. This is like being accused of bad spelling and having the reproach substantiated by the bare assertion that spelling rules exist. Without, therefore, going into the problem of whether or not reality should be reckoned with, we wish to consider another question: Can we formulate a general principle regulating the interrelationship between our knowledge of historical necessity and our moral convictions? Between the world of being and the world of values? Between reality and what ought to be? We formulate these preliminary observations to put an end to those pitiful controversies in which one side reveals triumphantly that reality must be reckoned with, and the other protests eagerly that it never intended to question that injunction.

---

counters availed himself of the arguments briefly summarized here in the dispute with the clerk.

But meanwhile, things have changed. One of the participants in that debate, who used to write under the pen name of Pawel Konrad, has in the meantime been withdrawn from historical circulation, having been murdered by the missionaries of great historical justice. The parties to today's discussion ought to remember this when they return to the arguments of ten years ago and repeat them intact. They should recall, I say, how possible it was—and therefore may be once again—to justify and sanction anything with generalities about historical necessity, political realism, and the existence of a single alternative to which the world is allegedly doomed.

The Opiate of the Demiurge

When Hitler's armies were on their triumphant march across Europe, there was probably not a single Pole who doubted that theirs were temporary successes destined to end very quickly in resounding defeat. Some drew this certainty from their conviction that God would miraculously rout the enemy army and would not allow a nation of believers to perish. Others derived it from their faith that justice must ultimately prevail, still others from their confidence in the genius of Winston Churchill, some from their trust in Joseph Stalin. No one had a sound rational basis for this opinion, but it was easily accounted for by a situation in which the monstrosities and horrors of daily life had reached such proportions that no one could imagine them to be a lasting reality, due to go on indefinitely. In countries where the Hitlerite occupation seemed somewhat less brutal, or at any rate where mass terror did not attain the scale it reached in Poland, an unshakable belief in Hitler's downfall was not nearly so universal.

There were people in the West who devised a new philosophy of history for the situation of the "New Europe," arguing that the Hitlerite state was indeed barbarous and monstrous, but that fate had doomed the world to fall prey to civilized savagery so that a new, humanitarian, and democratic civilization might arise later on the ruins of contemporary culture. Thus a historical cycle had been completed in which, as has repeatedly happened in history, great and mature civilizations lost their vitality and crumbled beneath the blows of barbarians, who in turn began to create history anew on that part of the earth. India's conquest by the Aryans, the Mycenaean culture, Greece, Rome . . . historical speculation finds much food for thought in ancient history. But practically, at that time, what was one to do? Practically, one was supposed to support Hitlerism, or at least allow it to carry out its work freely, in the name of historical necessity.

If such an attitude disgusts us, let us nonetheless consider what our revulsion is directed against. Is it directed against the mere fact of someone's doubting it was possible to beat Hitler? After all, at the beginning of 1942 it was very hard to prove by rational argument that the Third Reich was doomed to defeat. Even if we believe that universal historical laws govern changes in social patterns, knowledge of these laws is so vague that we cannot predict when and with what concatenation of circumstances— convulsions, wars, revolutions, vicissitudes of defeat and victory —one social pattern will be ousted by another. It is easy to display historiosophical wisdom about past events, but history usually scoffs at forecasts of the future. In any case, the over-throw of the Hitlerite state could not at that time be deduced from any historiosophical diagrams, nor could it, in the grave moments of the war, be cogently argued from the course of military operations. That defeat was not a foregone conclusion; it was fought for and won by the terrible striving and suffering of nations. Are there any laws of history that preclude the possibility of the fascist army's having been the first to possess thermo-nuclear weapons, and would it have hesitated to use them? In posing such questions, I have no intention of gibing or railing at people who, regardless of historiosophical considerations and often quite irrationally, cherished an unflinching certainty as to fascism's downfall—and this not because their conviction was eventually borne out, but mainly because in itself it constituted an essential ingredient of victory.

Even if in a particular situation sound common sense rebels against hope, understandably hope is more important than common sense to a fighting force; defeatism in an army may some-times be warranted by rational thinking, but we must recognize and accept the fact that it cannot be tolerated. We must also reconcile ourselves to the idea that an excess of common sense may be inimical to an effective fight, even a fight for a just cause. *Beati qui non viderunt et crediderunt.* (Blessed are those who did not see, and believed.) It is surely legitimate to silence a man who from rational premises foresees a setback for his own side in battle, because a conviction that one's efforts are futile makes them doubly so. This is an unfortunate contradiction of human existence that nothing can eliminate.

But for all that, you cannot forbid thinking. You cannot, therefore, prevent one person or another from taking a skeptical view of the prospects for his cause in the most violent fray. Sometimes, too, this skepticism proves justified; in any case, it is justified on one of the two embattled sides. After all, during the September campaign, no doubt of the lightning triumph of the Polish army over the invaders' "cardboard tanks" was permitted.

Thus we revert to the question raised earlier. If we rightly ask skeptics not to spread their doubts among others, still we cannot morally condemn someone for the fact that he has allowed doubt to crop up in his own mind. One could, I repeat, believe in the dark moments of the last war that victory would go to the Hitlerites. This supposition is not in and of itself subject to moral judgment; but the practical conclusions deduced from it and the attitude one takes to such a view of the world are. No one can be absolved of moral responsibility for supporting crime on the grounds that he was intellectually convinced of its inevitable victory. No one is relieved of the moral obligation to oppose a system of government, a doctrine, or a social order that he regards as base and inhuman by pleading that he considers it historically necessary. We are against that form of moral relativism which assumes that the criteria for a moral assessment of human behavior can be derived from knowledge of the secrets of the *Weltgeist*.

This is not a protest against the thesis that people's moral convictions actually depend on their social situation, but a protest exclusively against attempts at a normative interpretation of historiosophy—against the theory that duty derives from necessity, against a quest for moral criteria in the knowledge of historical laws, against a doctrine which, not content to judge the past MORALLY *by its effects on the present, evaluates the present by its results in the future, fancying it has a complete and infallible knowledge of what those results will be. This is a protest against the opinion that in historical clashes, even on the scale of the* Weltgeist, *victory will inevitably go to the just cause, meaning* that the just cause is precisely the one that wins. Thus the saying "The future belongs to the righteous" is reduced to a tautology, since whoever the future belongs to decides who is to be considered righteous.

Let us go into this matter more deeply. When a meteorologist foresees a hailstorm he doesn't say, "There will be a hailstorm. We can forecast it, but to forestall it is not in our power. The hailstorm is inevitable, therefore rejoice in it! Work up enthusiasm for the storm, sing hymns in its praise, and persuade the farmers that instead of protecting their crops against the hail, they should yearn for it to fall."

The historical prophet is in a different position. Above all, he knows in advance that human history aims toward progress—a word whose meaning is never really elucidated, it is true, but which roughly speaking should be perceived in the social consciousness as the designation of a series of situations each of which is "better" than its predecessor. Viewed on a sufficiently large scale, history is a progressive process. This means, in practical terms, that in general man is increasingly better off in this world.

It may happen, of course, that "man" is not easily convinced of this thesis. In that case, several possibilities present themselves. As a rule, one must note that in resisting it "man" exhibits a shallow empiricism; instead of penetrating the essence of things, which grows ever better, he busies himself with the trifles of his empirical existence, which do not show a like improvement. In this instance "man" is simply not philosophically well schooled. It may also happen that the "empirical ego" of the man we are considering conflicts objectively with the "absolute ego" of the social consciousness—that the man represents a regressive element in collective life. Finally, it may be that what "man" takes as a deterioration in the situation is merely a transitory phase leading to radical improvement—that we are dealing with a dialectical "step backward in order to make another leap forward." In any case, "man" must be persuaded that the world is moving toward something better, especially if we measure its development in sufficiently large segments of time.

Once he is convinced of this, the biggest difficulty ceases to exist. Now it suffices to demonstrate that a particular phenomenon occurred at the bidding of that great demiurge of history —progress—and thereby to show it to be a step in mankind's march toward a better world. By the same token, support of this event or situation becomes morally binding on all who have the good of mankind at heart.

What better criterion for moral judgment can we find than collaboration with the hidden workings of historical progress? To believe in the inevitability of progress is to believe in the progressive nature of everything that is inevitable as well. To believe in Providence is to bless the brick that lands on your head. When the spirit of history assumes the difficult role of Divine Providence, it must, like its model, exact humble gratitude for every slap in the face that it administers to its wards.

The demiurge of progress, who watches over the world, commands that he be extolled in all his creatures and all his images. And what is easier to prove than that this or that national leader, this or that system of government, this or that pattern of society is, though its ape-like exterior may frighten people, the anointed of the demiurge? After all, Catholic historians admit that God, wishing to test the faithful, now and again delivered St. Peter's See into the hands of the ungodly. So much greater, then, the merit of the faithful if they bow their heads to the Divine Voice, even though it issues from the throat of Balaam's she-ass. If the demiurge of progress deigns to speak as Genghis Khan, the more perspicacious the historiosopher, the sooner he offers his services to Genghis Khan. When zoologists come to the conclusion that the age of man has ended on the earth and the age of ants is approaching, the historiosopher will have no choice but to advise everyone to sit down voluntarily on ant heaps and leave their skeletons there. This will assuredly be useful to progress, once it has been established that progress is the law of history.

In truth, however, this is no laughing matter, and the predicament we are trying to find a way out of sometimes seems harder to understand rationally than the mystery of the Trinity. For the sake of greater clarity, let us take for granted one common assumption in the debate as well as two ideological extremes which, proceeding from that assumption, express in practice two opposite positions.

The common assumption is this: Socialism as an imagined rather than an actual pattern of social relations represents a certain complex of values, acknowledged and affirmed as such, which have a moral nature in the sense that their implementation presents itself as a moral duty. In other words, socialism furnishes a criterion, either universal or partial, for the assessment of men's actions.

Two extreme attitudes develop from this assumption: so-called ethical socialism, as we know it in history; and Stalinism, in the most profitable and purely ideological version we can formulate. Omitting the social sources and historical situations that may engender one or the other attitude, we shall consider them both in the realm of pure thought.

From the point of view that now concerns us, ethical socialism can be summarized as follows: socialism is the sum total of social values whose implementation is incumbent on the individual as a moral duty. It is a body of imperatives regarding human relations that an individual or a group sets itself. To what extent these values can actually be implemented is a question altogether distinct from that of whether one *ought* to work toward their realization. Duty, according to Kant's thesis, should be fulfilled because it is a duty and not because the actual results of our actions, in a world not entirely dependent on us, will or can really be what we desire. If we were convinced that socialism was impossible, our duty to fight for it would not dwindle or weaken; on the contrary, only then would our efforts acquire the halo of heroism that fully points up their moral worth. For to act morally means to act out of pure awareness of duty, from the pure imperative, regardless of whether reality will yield to our desires. Only he who fights knowingly for a lost cause can be free from suspicion of ulterior motives. He who joins the struggle for socialism sustained by an unwavering certainty of victory is merely betting on a number at which history's roulette wheel is, in his opinion, bound to stop. His actions are morally worthless, since they either aim at his being on the winning side in the struggle or are, at least in their motives, indistinguishable from sheer opportunism. It becomes difficult in this case to draw the line between investing one's efforts in an enterprise that will yield a high profit historically, and fighting for a cause deemed to be morally just.

The true socialist acts at the risk of losing, sometimes even with the certainty of losing; and the greater the probability of defeat, the higher the moral value of his deed. The duty to fight for socialism has no motivation other than the fact that it is a duty, which means that socialism is realized as a value of the individual's moral effort. Those who think that socialism is as inevitable in the future as an eclipse of the sun scheduled for tomorrow can find nothing to lend moral worth to deeds performed with an absolute certainty of success. Moreover, it is not true that such certainty can rouse anyone to action, for the goal in that case will be achieved "anyway," no matter how one person or another may act. Given such reasoning, a political party that sets out to fight for socialism while considering its advent inescapable is the party of the eclipse of the sun.

And that is the interpretation of the moral situation of a socialist according to Stalinist doctrine, presented, we repeat, in the most profitable version that can be devised: Socialism is historical inevitability. This means that all who try to prevent its coming will necessarily be beaten by those who struggle for the new order. It does not, however, mean that the victory will be won in any way except through the action of the masses of humanity. The laws of history will cause the masses to be pushed in just that direction necessary to end the existence of a society divided into classes. The moral worth of an individual's actions is gauged by his participation in this necessary process. Necessity is progress—that is the wager we make at the outset. If this is so, all action through which this necessity is realized is also progressive; there is really no difference between the expressions "historically progressive" and "morally good." To be more precise, a difference can exist, but only (though one doesn't talk about it) when one is dealing with propertied classes representing progress in a given historical epoch. The difference vanishes completely in the case of the working class carrying out its historical mission of abolishing a class society.

Once the proletariat comes to power, absolute harmony reigns between the moral worth of men's deeds and society's historical development. In other words, that which favors the evolution of a socialist society in accordance with its own laws is in these circumstances moral. Therefore it is moral to insure that the primacy of the production of means of production over the production of means of consumption is maintained; that agricultural production is collectivized; that the principle of economic planning works; that earnings are alloted according to work, etc.

The doctrinaire Stalinist is in an awkward position, however, and when confronted with certain questions is obliged to do some shamefaced shifting. He professes that "morally right" and "historically progressive" really mean the same thing. If we should ask—the question is rather unlikely to occur to him— whether, in the economically progressive process of the original accumulation of land in England, accomplished through the use of brute force and exploitation, each individual landowner who evicted the peasants deserved praise because he was doing the work of the *Weltgeist*, he will have two replies. The first will be that this is an academic question; the second, that there is an antagonism here. As a matter of fact, the word "antagonism" solves any number of difficult problems, for an internally contradictory theory is perfectly designed to preserve itself by saying that reality contains internal contradictions. Thus the principle of conflict immanent in the world is supposed to protect the doctrine from the charge of inconsistency. "On the one hand," economic progress in class societies is effected at the expense of the exploited classes; still, it is progress, therefore the *Weltgeist* is on its side. "On the other hand," those exploited classes are right in their opposition; and so the alter ego of the *Weltgeist* takes sides with them. A contradiction? But every contradiction in the doctrine is its triumph, for the world is based on contradictions. When the *Weltgeist* rebels against itself, the doctrinaire hoists his flag over its tattered soul: the rebellion only confirms his reason for being. The doctrinaire boasts of the consistency of his system, but whenever necessary, he also prides himself on its internal contradictions.

In any case, he adds at once, these contradictions pertain to class societies and vanish into thin air as soon as the new socialist society enters the stage of construction. Now the *Weltgeist* mends its torn soul once and for all; a simple relationship of identity prevails between what is morally right and what is economically progressive. Now the Stalinist ideologist triumphs as the champion of consistency. "There are no absolute and universally valid moral norms," he argues, "and if they should be proved to exist, they could forfeit their universality the moment they collided with the requirements of progress." To establish that a particular line of action favors social progress is the same thing as proving that it is a moral duty. In this manner we define values by relating them to progress.

But we cannot, in turn, relativize the concept of progress by referring back to moral values. If we wish to avoid the obvious trap of reasoning in circles, we must choose one of the two concepts—either social progress or moral values—as logically prior to the other. Should we attempt to define social progress in terms of values, we would be in danger, first, of endowing the concept of progress with a purely moral content, which is contrary to the assumptions of historical materialism. (The doctrinaire Stalinist rejects as scholastic and formalistic the idea that the genetic, historical interdependence of phenomena has nothing at all to do with which is the *determinant/definiens* and which the *determined/definiendum* in the theory.) Second, we would be in danger of recognizing certain moral values as absolutely binding regardless of historical events, which is contrary to dialectics. We have no way out of this predicament but to invert the order—to determine moral values by relating them to historical progress. The concept of progress must, therefore, shed its characteristic of evaluation and assume a purely "objective" substance. This means that progress in turn, must be defined as that which realizes the *Weltgeist*, or the laws of history, which are "ultimately" dependent on the development of the tools of production. And thus, to prove the moral validity of anything, one must establish it to be "ultimately" useful to the growth of technology. This usefulness is a condition both indispensable to and adequate for every appraisal; and the development of the means of production, since it acts as the *prime mover* of history, also acts as the *ultimate end* of human action. These elements of the vision of the world were identified centuries ago by theologians.

In this fashion a Marxism for those deficient in social theory is supplemented by a Hegelianism for those deficient in moral doctrine. Such an interpretation of socialist morality has found a following among some communists—those who are morally sensitive—who espouse it as an attempt to resolve the conflicts between their conscience and the social reality in which they find themselves. In innumerable instances Stalinism has repeated the spiritual history of young Belinski, who believed that Russian czardom embodied the spirit of history and that one should not resist history for foolish personal reasons but assent to its basic course despite the anxieties and resistance of the individual conscience. The moral problem of the individual was supposed to consist not in the application of his own yardstick of righteousness to historical events, but solely in the adaptation of his own sense of righteousness to historical inevitability. Once the individual sees himself as merely a tool of the general substance of history, his duty consists of assimilating the situation not only intellectually but also morally. That is to say, every reaction of moral revolt against what presents itself as historical necessity must be labeled an impulse of a tool trying—an inconceivable thing metaphysically —to change into an autonomous substance. Such an attempt to break away from historical necessity is not only doomed in advance, as the theory of the individual's role in history proves, but is also reprehensible because it is contrary to progress.

Those who accepted this philosophy of history tried with its aid to reconcile the actual reality of socialism with their idea of it. The *Weltgeist* helped in bridging the gap that separated the ideological substance of communism from all the crimes perpetrated in its name. This view of reality was not merely the prerogative of a handful of historiosophers speculating on man's fate, but also acquired sufficiently broad scope to qualify as a social phenomenon. The opiate of the *Weltgeist*, applied in a more or less vulgarized form, effectively desensitized consciences to the morally irksome stimuli of everyday life. The substance of history imposed its domineering primacy upon the subservient "tools," who were convinced that their hidden revulsions and unavowed reflexes of disgust were but normal exertions in the gigantic job of pulling the chariot of history. But the "tools" who accepted the theory of the *Weltgeist* and with its help whitewashed all the sinister spots of current reality, as well as their own opportunism, were by no means innocent dupes of a false historiosophy. Their original mistake was not in accepting historical destiny itself, with its liberation from moral responsibility and thereby their own liberation as its instruments. What is basic is that the communists who believed in the absolute amorality of history believed at the same time in the superfluousness of every morality capable of emancipating itself from history's demands, and that they took no interest in the substance of that historical necessity at whose doorstep they laid their own conformity. They never sought to ascertain or decide independently what did or did not constitute the content of that necessity, shifting the heavy burden of inquiring into the designs of the demiurge of history onto the shoulders of their superiors. They willingly agreed to let others divine the shrewd intentions of the *Weltgeist* and announce the results of their communion with it.

They passively accepted as historical necessity whatever they were talked into, and afterward carried out its alleged or real behests with good will. In the realm of the *Weltgeist*, they were simple retainers who paid their taxes to history without expecting the right to vote on its decisions or even a full knowledge of what those decisions might be. And they consented to this role without protest. The conflict between the real world and the world of recognized values manifested itself only in a subcutaneous cynicism, which acts always as a light antidote to the bitter taste of permanent conformity. For cynicism is but the clear awareness of the contradictions between one's own actions and the general values recognized in a given society and tacitly accepted by the cynic himself. That is why real criminals are not cynics. It is only here that we touch the sore point of the problem—the point mentioned at the beginning of these reflections.

How can the conviction that historical necessity exists and that it must be implemented by brutal and terrifying means be reconciled with the recognition of absolute values—with the belief that certain kinds of behavior are prescribed and others forbidden under all circumstances? Moral duty is the conviction, perpetuated in a given social setting, that certain types of actions are ends in themselves, not just means to an end, and others, in and of themselves, are anti-ends, that is to say, proscribed. If historical necessity is seen as an unlimited process without a defined final stage, or if an ultimate goal is attributed to it that has not yet been attained but constitutes merely a promise for the future, and if at the same time moral judgments are subordinated to the realization of historical necessity—then there is nothing at all in daily life that can be an end in itself. In other words, moral values in the strictest sense cease to exist. Can a vision of the world in terms of existence be reconciled with one in terms of value?

This is one version of the dispute between extreme political realism and extreme utopianism. We call extreme realism an individual's belief in the fundamental inevitability of the historical process —with all its details—in the midst of which it is his lot to live, as well as the belief in the futility of all attempts to set any moral postulates against current reality. Realism thus understood brands all moralizing about the existing world as sterile and utopian, and does so in the name of the demiurge of history which does not suffer moralists. On the other hand, utopianism in the sense we are using it consists in taking the attitude of a permanent critic of reality, in measuring reality exclusively against arbitrary yardsticks of good and evil. The sole protest of the utopian confronted by social reality is to assert that it is morally faulty; his sole means of influencing it, to tell people what the world *should* be in order to live up to those absolute criteria.

We assume that in the controversy between these two positions (and in order to avoid fruitless arguments about matters of fact we will simply present them as ideals, without illustrations) there are common assumptions. The realist does not question, for he need not, the moral values which the utopian seeks to oppose to current history. All he questions is the usefulness of any such opposition. In his turn the utopian does not question historical determinism; what he queries is anybody's right to judge events morally on the basis of an appraisal of their historical inevitability. For he is convinced that such moral judgments do not depend on a knowledge of whether the fact being assessed fits well or badly as a link in the historical chain outlined by a given philosophy of history. Moreover, the parties to this dispute upbraid each other for the lamentable practical effects of their respective attitudes. According to his antagonist, the realist, by advocating theoretical opportunism vis-à-vis history, is simultaneously a political opportunist in every actual situation. All he has instead of a program of changes is one of adjusting himself to the patterns he encounters. He accepts the world of things without demur because it is the only world that exists, and the sole world that might oppose it is that of values, which is a fiction gratuitously devised by dreamers and devoid of roots in nature. On the other hand, the utopian is, in the opinion of his opponent, precisely that builder of imaginary worlds who in practice dooms himself to sterility because he sets himself unattainable goals spun out of his own notions of perfection, thus preventing himself from achieving feasible ends based on an analysis of the possibilities contained in this world of nonmalleable and resistant things.

In this fashion the utopian-reformer-dreamer and the fatalist-realist argue with each other, and they have been arguing thus ever since people consciously set out to better their social existence—which means almost since the beginning of time. The discussion is rather like halloos from opposite banks of a river that cannot be swum. Between submissiveness to the world encountered and obedience to moral imperatives yawns an abyss on whose brinks the great tragedies of history have been enacted: tragedies of conspiracies and uprisings foredoomed to failure, and, across the chasm, those of collaboration with crime because of belief in its inevitability. It is on these two brinks that the moral drama of the revolutionary movement has been played in recent years.

Marx was the man who sought to build a bridge between the two cliffs, and on this bridge utopian socialism was essentially to be overcome. He summed up his view in the words: "We must force ossified attitudes to dance by humming their own tune to them," which is to say that people create their own history—not arbitrarily, but by yielding to the pressure of conditions. Marx devoted the greater part of his life to discovering that natural melody of history, and yet those who carried on his theoretical work were constantly obliged to reconsider this problem, to compose over and over a posthumous opera based on the unfinished manuscript of *Capital* and in the light of new experience to answer the same question: "What is to be done?" The two men who wrote books under this title, Chernyshevski and Lenin, represent two evolutionary phases of this persistent effort: the endless confrontation of current experience with a purely imaginary ideal, the continuous dialogue between reality as it is and a reality that is only dreamed of.

The difficulty of this job is not the ordinary one of discussing a theoretical problem which has not yet found a sufficiently well-based answer, but which may arrive at it some day, when the issue will be settled once and for all. Here we face a question which can never be finally resolved in a manner applicable to all the accidents of history, but must be tackled anew for every actual historical situation that occurs—for each is new, each is nonrecurrent, and none are susceptible of analysis merely by invoking analogies from the past.

This is due to the fact that historical determinism is by nature vague. By "determinism" I mean a doctrine describing the regularities of social changes, to which it ascribes validity for the future. Marx's predictions referred to changes in economic patterns and were formulated with that scale in mind; his natural scientific criticism did not permit that further particularization which so delighted Fourier and the majority of utopians. The programs that Lenin formulated before the October Revolution went considerably further in detail, yet we cannot be sure what parts of these programs were based on peculiarly Russian conditions and what were, or at least were intended to be, universally valid for the transition period from capitalism to socialism. We can certainly grant that Marx's basic assumption that the progress of capitalist technology engenders a tendency to impose collective forms of ownership on means of production is, by and large, corroborated by history.

But through how many lost and won revolutions, how many wars and crises, after how many years or decades, in what chronological or geographical configurations, through what regressions and upsurges, and in what various forms a socialist society will arise—this is precisely what cannot be deduced cogently from a general knowledge of "the laws of history." These questions are answered empirically by everyday life, which, like a skillful magician, daily startles us with fresh surprises. On the whole, these circumstances do not disturb historiosophers; they are quite content in the knowledge that they have spent years toiling over the same epitaph for capitalist society, writing it, in their opinion, on the basis of "scientific prediction." As for those wars, revolutions, crises, decades of fighting and suffering, they fall into the philosophical category of "accidents" and are for that reason free, not subject to penetrating historiosophical analysis. Of the mysteries of the spirit of history, historiosophers possess knowledge about the ultimate point at which history's peregrinations will cease, while the tortuous paths it stumbles along toward its goal escape their prophetic eye. Each stage traveled—and the word "stage" (*étape*) may aptly be used here in the same sense that it measured the journeys of the czars' stagecoaches—can be interpreted causally once it has been completed, and in enough different ways to supply historiosophers with themes for many years' deliberations and arguments; but rarely is any one of them foreseen. That is why they have been called "accidents"—a word which over the centuries has raised man's indolence to the status of a theory, and which in our time, no less effectively than in Spinoza's, constitutes an "asylum of ignorance." Nevertheless, historiosophers will never lack the courage to devise, on just such a knowledge of the world's destiny, practical regulations that are binding upon every individual and that morally compel him to collaborate with the march of history.

Nothing discourages historiosophy. At every turn of history that lays bare its impotence, it blows fanfares of triumph; it even carries out self-criticism to a martial air played on trumpets and bugles. Its admirable fortitude in the face of cruel defeats is obviously traceable, not to innate soundness, but to the fact that it is itself a tool of the "shrewd wisdom" of history, which begets historiosophy to beguile the social consciousness, deceiving it with unthinking opportunism and commanding it to believe that having shed all illusions it sees reality as an open book. Demythologizing has itself become a myth, and therefore, although events may belie historiosophy at every step, it is still able to present its setbacks as victories, just as the Delphic Oracle always turned out to be right. Historiosophy draws its strength not from itself but from the faith people have in it; this faith is part and parcel of political practice and its character is semisacred. The most tattered and torn cloak can assume the aspect of a royal robe if donned by a priest whom the people worship. Those who prophesy from dreams will never be shaken in their belief by the mere fact that it has been empirically proved that dreams do not necessarily come true, for they always have one or two examples at hand to illustrate the contrary and prop their faith. Faith needs no justification, but only illustration and sanction.

Yet we need no longer jeer at historiosophy. However meager its possibilities, it does have certain modest merits that cannot be disputed, even if this man or that or possibly the whole social system should make it an instrument of moral masochism. We are all the less free to treat it contemptuously since these reflections belong essentially to its domain and are meant to enrich its Potemkin Villages. Accordingly, we may observe also that thinking in historiosophical terms has spread to such an extent and has taken on such proportions that with the best will in the world it is impossible to dislodge it from social life in favor of a naked empiricism whose horizons are limited to dawn and dusk. The dawns and dusks not of single days but of great epochs and historical patterns have become the daily bread of human thought, and to seek to deprive countless people of the privilege of beholding the world from the lofty heights of great history is a game not worth the candle. Such a situation alone is enough to induce one unable to deprive others of the delights of historiosophy to partake of its benefits himself. This, then, is the excuse for the present discussion, which we now wish to bring to a decisive phase.

Conscience and Social Progress

In the dispute between realism and utopianism, the arguments against the latter have been formulated so often and in such detail that I need not repeat them. I shall, however, submit some "antirealist" propositions which for certain reasons seem especially significant.

These premises are the following:

FIRST ASSUMPTION: *ethical individualism. Only human beings and their deeds are subject to moral judgment.* There can be no moral evaluation without consideration of the intentions of the acting agent, and intentions can be ascribed only to men. From this, in turn, one must infer that it is impossible to evaluate morally the good or bad results of an anonymous historical process. It is equally impossible to make a moral assessment, in the strict sense of the word, of a group or social class, if by a social class we mean—and this definition seems to us appropriate—not only a collection of individuals but a social "entity," a body which behaves in such a way that the reactions of the human elements which compose it are governed by the class as a whole and not vice versa.

It is important to stress that this does not imply that membership in a specific class or group—and, in general, this rather than any other kind of dependence in which every individual finds himself vis-à-vis the society in which he lives—is not decisive in determining both his moral opinions and the part of his behavior which is subject to moral judgment and which has been very differently circumscribed over the centuries. On the contrary, we assume hypothetically—although we lack sufficient proof—that this determination is absolute. (I mean social determination and not determination resulting exclusively from membership in a class.) And we formulate this as our:

SECOND ASSUMPTION: *determinism.* Opinions about good and evil and about the morality of people's behavior are determined by the way an individual participates in society. Under "participation" we include upbringing and the influence of tradition, as well as membership in all the social groups from whose confluence arises that unique thing called personality. (Of course tradition is also a social group, namely, a totality of people who remain within the sphere of influence of a given form of consciousness shaped before their time.)

We shall not dwell here on such questions as what share different forms of social life have in the molding of moral views; how many stem from universal aspects of social life and therefore assume an "elementary" nature of universal validity; how many derive from conditions particular to a class society and thus acquire, in any case, extreme longevity; and finally, which ones result from membership in a specific class, in a profession, and so on. (These questions summarize the main problems of the sociology of morality and, as such, lie outside the framework of this essay.)

Although many moralists hold these two assumptions to be contradictory, we maintain they are not. There is no logical contradiction between social determinism even more rigorously conceived than in our usage of the term, and the acceptance of moral responsibility. This results from the next premise:

THIRD ASSUMPTION: *the humanistic interpretation of values.* Although a given person may accept the fact that his moral values and behavior are determined, nevertheless he cannot infer from his knowledge of the conditions that determine him any conclusions concerning the truth or falseness of values he has accepted. In other words, the fact that a person knows he judges something to be good or bad because specific circumstances inclined him to do so does not mean that this something is good or bad. Everyone has moral opinions, but he cannot justify them by claiming they result from certain ascertainable outside causes. Furthermore, to state that an individual can be judged morally means that *the right to judge him* has been given to others. This is a normative statement and consequently its negation is also normative. Thus when we affirm that the principle of determinism, which is a theoretical formula, proves that moral responsibility is impossible, we tacitly assume that moral values can be deduced from purely theoretical propositions. If we reject the possibility of this deduction, we are forced to admit that the question of determinism or nondeterminism of human activity has no logical connection with the confirmation or denial of man's moral responsibility, for neither the affirmation nor the denial is a theoretical proposition. In this manner our third assumption removes the supposed contradiction between our first two.

The third premise, therefore, would let us keep the concept of moral responsibility completely independent of our knowledge, or rather our postulates, about social or any other determination of human behavior, even if that knowledge were incomparably greater than it now is. Actually, it is rather meager in regard to individual cases, though it may be verifiable in general on a broad scale.

To say that an individual is morally responsible for his actions implies that his social environment has the right to make a moral evaluation of his acts and to approve or disapprove. It further implies that the environment is aware of this right. These reactions are as determined as the very act to which they apply. To deny society this right is to judge its reactions morally and therefore to act in a manner proscribed by the content of our action, in other words, to fall into a practical contradiction. We would then find ourselves in the situation of a Carthusian prior who loudly berates his brethren for breaking the vow of silence, or of someone who asks the death penalty for all who demand that the death penalty be retained.

Denying society the "right" to approve or condemn is somewhat like decreeing that earthquakes may not occur or that rain may not fall. In this respect we follow the ideas of Spinoza. The existence of the social fact that individuals are judged according to their moral behavior must be accepted in the same spirit as we accept natural laws. Superficially this seems to contradict what we said before. For we demand that the moral responsibility of the individual be recognized, and therefore we grant society the right to a moral judgment. In a way, we agree not to question the rain's right to fall and then proceed to affirm positively that it does have this right. This places us in a difficulty that arises not from the content of the evaluation but from the fact that this evaluation was expressed. In reality, these two situations are not entirely analogous, because the person who grants society a specific right in the matter under consideration himself belongs to this society. By conceding this right to society he grants it to himself as well, and to some extent he becomes the voice of society.

Moral judgment is not, obviously, an act of "pure" cognition—if that exists at all—a passive acknowledgment of a certain view of things; it is a verbal formulation of a practical initial attitude toward a situation that is subject to moral evaluation. That things "in themselves" are neither good nor evil, but are only experienced as such, is a truth that has been restated over the centuries from Aenesidemus and the Sophists, through Hobbes and Spinoza, to Schlick and Carnap, so we may skip the arguments in favor of this thesis. However, our acceptance of it does not mean that we must renounce moral judgments, which would be an act reminiscent of the practical contradiction described above. On the contrary, we assume that the deterministic theory, whether accepted or rejected, cannot in any case logically support or violate this type of proposition, for one belongs to the world of knowledge and the other to the world of duty. When we affirm the existence of moral responsibility, questions about the nonambiguity, nature, or very existence of the determinism to which human behavior is subject, are not involved at all.

Our first assumption means that when we make statements such as "This historical process is progressive" or "This social class represents historical progress, but that one obstructs it," we are not voicing *moral* judgments though we are in some way evaluating the object under observation. It is another kind of evaluation, which obviously assumes certain criteria of improvement, human benefit, development, and the like. Indeed, if we were to seek criteria of social progress *exclusively* in the consequences of a given historical phenomenon (a practice I do not recommend)—for example, in the realm of the growth and spread in society of moral attitudes which we wish to propagate—even then a judgment of "historical progressiveness" would not be a moral judgment, although it contains a *priori* acceptance of a certain scale of moral values. It is one thing to say that a given kind of behavior is morally repugnant; it is quite another to establish that a certain historical process is progressive because it will lead to the reduction of this reprehensible behavior in society. Condemning the theft of public property is a different matter from proclaiming that a rise in prosperity is socially progressive because it obviates the need to steal. In the first instance we are formulating an explicit general moral concept; in the second we are really postulating a datum. But we do not apply it to a general social process since theft is committed only by individuals, not by living standards, technical development, or legislation. Individuals are the object of moral judgment, the rest are the objects of historical judgment.

This means that the three assumptions admit as a noncontradictory situation (although they do not logically entail it) one in which certain concrete human behavior must be judged negatively as to its morality and positively as to its role in the historical process, and vice versa. For the time being let us disregard the question of whether such situations occur in reality, and merely observe that they are possible since the two judgments are independent of each other. They are possible even if we postulate purely moralistic criteria of progress, which in my opinion would be wrong. Indeed, a situation could arise in which systematic thievery would favor social changes which would lead to the disappearance of theft as a social phenomenon.

Thus we return to the Hegelian problem, or more exactly, to the problem which derives from the interpretations of Hegel by all those who were influenced by his historical vision. Does the possession of a theory of progress replace or negate a simultaneous, noncontradictory use of criteria of moral behavior different from the criteria of historical progress? We are not interested now in whether some interpretations of Hegel are correct or not, but in the content of this question as fixed by post-Hegelian philosophy.

"The laurels of good intentions are dry leaves that never were green"—these words conclude the 124th paragraph of the *Philosophy of Law,* which ridicules those who seek to deprive great historical figures of their greatness and dignity on the grounds of their base motivations. In reality, their greatness and dignity are judged according to the role they played in the growth of the spirit of the times, which may utilize as a powerful weapon one man's desire for fame and respect, another's thirst for riches and conquest. Motives are immaterial when it comes to evaluating actions, since it is not the nobility or baseness of motivations that is being judged, but only the results of actions in the evolution of history.

This position contains nothing to negate the assumptions formulated above. Marx was in total agreement with the observation that the "progressiveness" or "backwardness" of historical processes or individual actions can be evaluated quite apart from any moral revulsion or approval they may generate. Let us take the liberty of citing his comments on the British colonization of India, in which he expounds this point of view: "Although human feelings recoil at the sight of the destruction and disintegration of tens of thousands of industrious, patriarchal, and peaceful social organizations cast into a sea of misfortune, at the sight of their members deprived simultaneously of their old civilization and their inherited means of livelihood—we must not, however, forget that these idyllic rural communities, despite their innocent appearance, had always been a strong basis of oriental despotism, that they restricted the human mind within the narrowest limits and made it into a tool of prejudice, an obedient slave of traditional principles, depriving it of all greatness and historical activity . . . that these small communities were torn asunder by divisions of caste and by slavery, that they surrendered man to the yoke of external conditions instead of making him ruler of them . . ." etc. And then the question: "Can humanity fulfill its mission without a radical revolution in Asian social relations? If not, then *regardless of even her greatest crimes, England was an unconscious tool of history in achieving this revolution.*

"Only after the great social revolution takes possession of the attainments of the bourgeois era, the world market and modern forces of production, and places them under joint control of the most advanced nations, only then will the progress of mankind se to resemble that hideous heathen god who refused to drink nectar except from the skulls of murdered men."

It would be difficult to express more succinctly the idea that concerns us. Though the values of historical progress are realized through crimes, they do not cease to be values nor do the crimes cease to be crimes. Similarly, great masterpieces of art do not lose their greatness because of the artists' base motives. It is possible that Plato's aesthetic was rooted in homosexuality. Possibly Dostoevski's genius thrived on his epileptic euphoria. It is conceivable that one can find traces of schizophrenia on a Van Gogh canvas and that syphilis stimulated Wyspianski's artistic outbursts. . . . Psychoanalysts and partisans of a physiological theory of art disclose any number of similar truths, cunningly assuming the air of courageous destroyers of what is sacred, as if to say: Look at your great men now! In fact, since Plato's aesthetic appeals to heterosexual people, since Dostoevski's writings charm non-epileptics, and nonsyphilitics read Wyspianski, what better proof is there that these disclosures are irrelevant when it comes to judging art? If excellent cheese is produced in dung, both the cheese and the manure retain their nature regardless of the causal relation between them.

This whole matter may seem banal, yet it presents great difficulties in the area that interests us. Marx's appraisal of the revolutionary role of British colonization by no means indicates that he had *moral* respect for British soldiers in India. If in many countries the industrial revolution was based on the massive use of slave labor, this does not mean that the slave owner deserves moral praise.

In other words, there is no reason to treat morality as the tool of history, in the sense of being obliged to seek criteria of moral good or bad in the realization of general historical progress. Crimes which were the tools of the *Weltgeist* are nevertheless crimes. Of course it is easy for us to accept this point of view with reference to the past. Thanks to its remoteness, the past does not evoke violent moral reactions, and we can formulate moral judgments almost as easily as simple statements of fact. With the present and the very recent past, this is more difficult, and not merely because our moral reactions are more immediate. Moral judgments may consist of applying an abstract yardstick of rectitude to a given fact (like reading a thermometer); if instead they are direct feelings, then natural conflicts arise when one must recognize certain facts as both morally repulsive and historically progressive.

But this is a purely psychological difficulty. Far more trouble in evaluating current events starts with the fact that it is precisely these that are hardest to judge as to their "historical progressiveness"; this characteristic emerges more clearly—though by no means unambiguously—when the event is drowned in the well of the past, or is considered from a distant perspective and in the context of many of its actual consequences. The present, in this respect, is always ambiguous and misty. This ambiguity creates particular hazards when we try to separate the two judgments—historical and moral—or when we give up the latter for the sake of the former. We know the past better than the present because we always see it in organized form, whereas the present is chaotic.

This problem appeared simultaneously with Hegel, that is, with the faith that mankind possessed a universal passkey of historical foresight, the key of David which unlocks all the secrets of the future (except for those "accidents" we have spoken of, which can harass the life span of several generations). Hegel was actually the first to outline, in his famous *Philosophy of History* and elsewhere, the possibility of omitting, in a *general historical analysis*, the individual human actions which comprise the growing process of man's world; more precisely, he originated the conviction that history cannot be written with the exclusive help of conceptual categories that describe individual human acts, passions, strivings, and fancies. For people "achieve what they want, but in the process something more is created which actually is inherent in what they want, but which did not exist in their minds or intentions."

This is the problem caused by the endless mutual interference of the two forms of awareness that have existed from the moment the concept of "historical progress" became a universal phrase. We experience history as our daily life; we observe history as the march of the spirit of the times. The constant confrontation of these two different approaches causes painful grimaces and troubled eyesight, as when a lens goes out of focus when the object being viewed moves abruptly.

As a result of Marx's theoretical work, at least some of the characteristics of the interpretation of history as a whole have become common knowledge. Almost no one believes any longer that the sole task of history is to act like the Lame Devil: ripping the roofs off human dwellings and watching people in their beds, in slippers, at their private safes; or opening their skulls in a search for hidden motives, passions, and plans. The general public now shares an awareness, not of historical laws, but of history as an independent object of reflection different from that constituted by the behavior of particular human beings. The latter is not the raw material of historical study, not *materia prima* ready to be shaped by general concepts and categories, but rather something which still demands causal interpretation in terms of the tendencies of human collectives.

Because of this, the problem which interests us is not only not solved, it is compounded. If it is true that one has to explain the behavior of individuals by historical processes and not vice versa, the fact remains that he who has assimilated this truth continues to be merely an individual who must, at every step, make basic choices and who receives from that general knowledge no efficient tools to help him choose. A moral choice does not become easier because one is aware either of its being determined, in the popular sense of the word, or of the fact that each component of the alternative is part of a historical perspective. More precisely, the choice will not be easier until we imagine that we have an infallible and ultimate knowledge of the laws of historical development, or that we have made the future of the world as dependable as a railroad schedule. Only when we fall victim to this mad illusion can we choose with facility, but at what a price! The price is that the absurdity of everyday life is *apparently* overshadowed by the fact that each of its phenomena is fictitiously elevated to the dignity of a general historical category and becomes the expression of one of the *universals* which compose our cosmic vision.

By its nature daily life is a torment, because no links exist between disparate events. It is an accumulation of individual situations which have in common only the fact that some of them resemble some others in some respects. Because of this, we are able to elaborate certain automatisms and habits which select our reactions in a manner that is superficially orderly but actually unthinking and customary. In fact, however, every particle of daily life exhausts itself and disappears faster than we can record it, and, together with the others, forms that dreadful void where nothing is real, nothing is really experienced, and everything dissolves into a chaotic mass of details. Consisting of separate phenomena without substantive connections, everyday life searches for bonds in accidentally adopted mythologies labeled "purposes in life." Any individual "purpose in life" is supposed to create a substance which will make every separate fact seem a "modus," thus conferring an appearance of authenticity on the flow of those daily happenings that actually pass before they can be fixed in the consciousness and leave behind them a feeling of absurdity. This attempt to give one's own life some semblance of substantiality, some external luster of consistency and unity organized by a single goal, may occasionally ease the pain of a life oppressed by the nightmare of its own senselessness.

These individual aims in life, these ephemeral mythologies that crumble at the slightest blow, can be replaced by the iron fortress of a philosophy of history. A consciousness permeated by the knowledge of historiosophy, which unerringly judges all facts in reference to general "laws" and unfailingly penetrates the future, can organize daily life admirably—as if it were a magnificent edifice in which every stone has a perfectly defined function and each is classified in general and very respectable categories. Each fact of everyday life merely serves to illustrate a theoretical category. The heap of disorderly impressions which previously constituted our existence is suddenly transformed into a paradise of neat universals. From the hell of scattered tatters of events we proceed into a charmingly symmetrical universe where only symbols and ideas exist. In this world there are no individuals, only expressions of ideas with their species stamped on their foreheads. In this world we no longer eat bread and butter but engage in the act of reconstituting our strength to work consciously toward the goal of building socialism. We do not sleep, we regenerate the gray cells in order to use them creatively in implementing the *Weltgeist*. We do not talk with men but with envoys of ideas, which in their turn are delegates of certain conflicting social forces in the gigantic march of history; and our words are but echoes of ideas. Every step has a definite direction, that of historical progress, whose plans we have discovered and whose goals are plain to everybody.

In this manner we move from the morass of daily existence into the madness of abstract life, as from a brothel into a monastery. The social sense of morality oscillates between these two extremes, both of which are unmasked sooner or later as the same idiotic life of illusion. It is quite understandable that the defeat of one of these means of assimilating life immediately urges the acceptance of the other, a phenomenon which can easily be observed in the most humdrum cases.

But since we do not intend at the moment to deal with all the forms of absurdity that crop up in life, let us turn our attention to one in particular: How can we free the morality of everyday life from the nightmare of historiosophy? How can we liberate it from that pseudodialectic which makes morality a tool of history and then makes history a pretext for villainy? We may make one reservation: We are not interested in that trivial criticism which attacks the historiosophical concept for "dehumanizing" the world by classifying the events of daily life theoretically. In spite of everything, this illusory heaven of ideas in which a consciousness educated by historiosophy thrives is nevertheless more human and less idiotic than that typical daily life filled, in the words of Julian Tuwim, "with misery during the week and with boredom on Sunday."

For the danger of constructing a morality within a historiosophical vision, and therefore meaningful only in that framework, does not lie in the attempt to interpret one's life as a fragment of history so as to give it, though arbitrarily, a sense it does not have in and of itself. The danger consists in the total replacement of moral criteria by criteria of the profit which the demiurge of history derives from our actions; and this threat increases the surer we are of knowing his intentions and plans. The spirit of sectarianism is the natural enemy of skepticism, and skepticism, though difficult to distribute, is the best possible antidote against the mad fanaticism of visionaries. This age-old truth should be recalled whenever historical experiences that make it particularly obvious repeat themselves.

When one attains an unshakable and absolute certainty that heaven is just around the corner, that Joachim da Fiore's "third order" is nearing its moment of triumph, and that final consolidation of the new era of history is imminent—the one that will "really" bring happiness, the one that is "really" different, the one that will crush the snake's head and put an end to human suffering—when, that is, we are obsessed by an unbounded conviction that we are on the threshold of paradise, then no wonder that one messianic hope becomes the unique governor of life, the sole source of moral precepts and the only measure of virtue. A consistent messianist must not hesitate to perform any task that may hasten the advent of the new era. Morality speaks then with the voice of the Apocalypse; it "sees a new heaven and a new earth"; and it knows that before the other bank is reached four angels will destroy a third of mankind, flaming stars will fall, an abyss will open up and seven cups of God's wrath will spill over the earth, and glory will crown the conqueror who slays the heathen with an iron rod. This apocalyptic philosophy of history, which Joachim da Fiore and Thomas Münzer expounded, found its way in a certain form into the communist movement. Although in the latter it was supported by honest and fertile scientific analysis, in practice it acted upon the mass movement as a messianic vision. Certainly it could not have been otherwise, but this acknowledgment cannot comfort us, since what we want to demonstrate is precisely the fact that we cannot deduce rules for our behavior from a more or less trustworthy knowledge of what is necessary in history.

At any rate, let us note as a practical rule that we need a certain amount of skepticism toward any prophetic philosophy of history that foresees the future with too much certitude. Experience teaches us that the enslavement of men by a historical process independent of them—the enslavement Marx described—has not decreased.

On the other hand, history is not merely a remote, indifferent force like the gods of Epicurus, but a series of situations that we are concretely engaged in independently of our will. If this involvement is a voluntary act of the individual, then it is also a moral act, at least in the sense that some values accepted in other circumstances come to the fore here as decisive factors.

Our question, therefore, may be formulated thus:

Since the morality of everyday life cannot be deduced from our knowledge of real or alleged historical necessities, must we advocate the defense of certain moral values recognized arbitrarily or assimiliated from tradition even if, in our opinion, history is turning against them? If we relinquish a morality based entirely on history, should we then promulgate an antihistorical morality?

We may answer:

Real social involvement is moral involvement. For although a great political movement that seeks to shape the world in its own image is called to life by the world's needs, and though its fundamental direction is determined by the development of social relations, nevertheless each individual's participation in any specific form of political life is a moral act for which that individual is wholly responsible.

No one is relieved of either positive or negative responsibility on the grounds that his actions formed only a fraction of a given historical process. A soldier is morally responsible for a crime committed on the orders of his superior; an individual is all the more responsible for acts performed—supposedly or in fact—on the orders of an anonymous history. If a thousand people are standing on a river bank and a drowning man calls for help, it is almost certain that one of the spectators will leap in to save him. This quasi-statistical certainty concerns a thousand people, but it does not eliminate the need for a moral evaluation of the specific person, that one in a thousand, who does jump into the river. Experience can assure us that one such man will be found in the crowd; and this certitude is analogous to those rare historical predictions that occasionally come true. But to be that precise person who, out of a thousand potential rescuers, carries out the prediction, which was based on large numbers, one must perform "by oneself," as it were, an action subject to moral judgment. By analogy, if there exists a social system which requires criminals for certain tasks, one can be sure it will always find them. But it does not follow that every individual criminal is absolved of responsibility, because in order to designate oneself for the role of such a tool of the system one must be a scoundrel "by oneself," one must voluntarily perform a specific act which is subject to moral judgment.

Thus we profess the doctrine of total responsibility of the individual for his deeds and of the amorality of the historical process. In the latter we avail ourselves of Hegel; in the former of Descartes. It was he who formulated the famous principle, whose consequences are not always visible at first glance, "There is not a soul so weak that it cannot, with good guidance, gain an absolute mastery over its passions." This means that we cannot explain away any of our actions on the grounds of emotion, passion, or the moral impotence to act differently, and that we have no right to transfer the responsibility for our conscious acts to any factor which determines our behavior; because in every instance we have the power to choose freely.

This assumption—which, as I have mentioned, can be accepted without contradicting the deterministic interpretation of the world—must also be extended to all the justifications we find for ourselves in historical necessities and historical determinism. Neither our personal, supposedly invincible emotions ("I could not resist the desire"), nor anyone's command ("I was a soldier"), nor conformity with the customs of one's environment ("everybody did it"), nor theoretically deduced exigencies of the demiurge of history ("I judged I was acting for the sake of progress") —none of these four most typical and popular rationalizations has any validity. This is not to say that these four types of determination do not actually occur in life, but merely to state that none of them releases us from individual responsibility, because none of them destroys the freedom of individual choice. Individual action remains in the absolute power of the individual. We walk the main roads of our life on our own:

> Not I, not anyone else can travel that road for you
> You must travel it for yourself. . . .
>
> —Whitman

I stress that we are concerned with *moral* responsibility. The soldier who executes his commander's erroneous orders—orders which are inefficient as military tactics—is not thereby responsible for the loss of the battle. A soldier who, on orders, participates in the mass murder of civilians is responsible for homicide. His moral duty is to not carry out the command. Only on this basis were we able to try SS men.

That is why, regardless of what philosophy of history we may wish to accept, we will be rightly judged for everything subject to moral appraisal that we do in its name.

And it is not true that our philosophy of history decides our main choices in life. They are determined by our moral sense. We are not communists because we recognized communism to be a historical necessity. We are communists because we stand on the side of the oppressed against their oppressors, on the side of wretches against their masters, on the side of the persecuted against their persecutors. Although we know that a theoretically correct division of society is not between "rich" and "poor" or "persecuted" and "persecutors," still when we have to accompany our theories with an act of *practical* choice, which means a *pledge*, then we act out of moral motivations, not theoretical concerns. It cannot be otherwise, for the most convincing theory is unable to make us lift our little finger. Practical choice is a choice of values, that is, a moral act, and that means an act for which everyone bears his own, personal responsibility.

History and Hope

Practical choices in this world are defined by "duty" and not by "existence." These two categories of *Sollen* and *Sein* characterize two attitudes and two visions of reality between which, with constant interruptions, we try to establish contact. The same question recurs repeatedly in different versions: How can we prevent the alternatives of *Sollen-Sein* from becoming polarizations of utopianism-opportunism, romanticism-conservatism, purposeless madness versus collaboration with crime masquerading as sobriety? How can we avoid the fatal choice between the Scylla of duty, crying its arbitrary slogans, and the Charybdis of compliance with the existing world, which transforms itself into voluntary approval of its most dreadful products? How to avoid this choice, given the postulate—which we consider essential—that we are never able to measure truly and accurately the limits of what we call "historical necessity"? And that we are, consequently, never able to decide with certainty which concrete fact of social life is a component of historical destiny and what potentials are concealed in existing reality.

For the sake of a more detailed reply to this question, we accept the following premises:

FOURTH ASSUMPTION: *the historical interpretation of value. Duty is a form of existence*. This means that by the very fact of its having assumed a social character, a moral feeling becomes part of the historical process and a factor that influences its course. Moreover, the conviction of a definite duty becomes an objective need of society. Many social views of what is correct are reflected in the social consciousness, not as theoretical knowledge, but as value judgments: this or that is "good" or "evil" morally, this or that "ought" or "ought not" to be done. If, unlike the positivist writers, we do not choose to be satisfied with deliberations about the specific language in which moral opinions are

143

expressed, and if we do not wish to take as the end of our knowledge the truth that normative statements cannot be deduced
from rules of logic—and if we therefore refuse to content ourselves
with the trivial cognizance that no theory of the universe suffices,
in and of itself, to construct a valid theory of values—then we
must consider the knowledge of both social phenomena and the
world of values as manifestations of collective life which in different ways reflect its laws, tendencies, and needs. In adopting
this approach we are not so much concerned with the question of
whether specific statements of moral evaluation are subject to the
dichotomy between falsehood and truth just like other judgments,
although we share the positivists' opinion that they are. We are
more interested, instead, in the connection that exists between
these two forms of the same social process, the consciousness of
values and theoretical consciousness. In reality, though, embar-
rassing as it is to say so, theories of social phenomena are all too
often only masked ideologies. This means that they are often
(although not always) a collection of values imposed on society
disguised as disinterested, scientific knowledge. But a sense of
values, to the degree it takes on social proportions—and the
criteria that establish when it does are, so far, difficult to fix—
is a distorted perception of certain facts of social life, of certain
of its concepts of what is correct, reflected in the crooked mirror
of special interests. If a given norm, though never entirely abided
by, is widely acknowledged, then the very fact of its existence
testifies that the needs of society, or of an important segment of it,
require that limits to the violation be set. *"Duty" is but the voice
of a social need.* In this sense the world of values is not merely an
imaginary sky over the real world of existence, but also a part of
it, a part that exists not only in the social consciousness, but that
is rooted in the material conditions of social life. From this we
derive the following:

FIFTH ASSUMPTION: *the negation of the pseudorealistic criticism of moralist utopias.* A social movement which supports its
program with moral justifications does not admit its failure merely
because its moral postulates have little chance of becoming concrete in the foreseeable future. It is a banality, whose truth

everyone experiences personally every day, that social systems fighting under attractive slogans graced with a moral halo resemble the content of these slogans very slightly. In other words, we should be wise enough not to be deceived by the prospect of a speedy coming of the kingdom of heaven. Yet it seems that we lack that wisdom—though superficially it does not appear to require excessive mental effort—and as a result, our mother—history —sometimes deals us blows that are doubly painful because we season them with mockery and with an awareness of our own naïveté.

Nevertheless, the fact is that the effects of the perennially discouraging experiences of the past are hardly felt by each succeeding generation; only its own experiences penetrate its consciousness. This fact, which at first glance speaks badly of the human species, is, on closer inspection, a wise and well-planned defense mechanism of nature. Achieving even the simplest improvement in social conditions demands the mobilization of such a huge amount of collective energy that if the full extent of the disproportion between results and effort expended became public knowledge the result would be so disheartening, and would so paralyze men's courage and strivings, that any social progress would be impossible. The effort must be so great as to be wasteful if the results are to be at all visible. In probably every living species the total quantity of seed must be a million times greater than the amount needed for procreation and survival. There is no reason why an analogous proportion should not govern social life, particularly since this is not a question of simple reproduction, but of evolution and perfection. No wonder, then, that in order to muster the energy needed to arrive at any change in human relations, this monstrous disproportion must be largely mitigated in men's minds by an artificial and mythological inflation of expected results as compared to the sum of expended effort, a sum which cannot be concealed since it is felt directly. Such distortions, which at first seem to border on fantasy, are actually the products of an ideology that for this very reason becomes an indispensable factor in social progress. Ideologies create mirages of distant lands to summon the exertions necessary for the caravan, though in distress, to reach the nearest oasis. If these enticing fata morganas did not loom up, the weary column, depressed by its hopeless situation, would let itself be buried in the desert sands.

If the disparity between our present situation and the improvement we are really in a position to achieve is very slight, and the effort needed to attain it is gigantic, then the natural device which falsifies the ratio is very useful. It is also useful on the assumption that, in spite of everything, it "pays" to fight for the difference. Since these differences constitute social progress, the answer to whether the effort "pays" is a foregone conclusion. There is simply no other possibility. Besides, these matters are unmeasurable, they absolutely cannot be counted like profits from investments. To be more precise, the question of whether social progress "pays" has no clear meaning. Because it is impossible to measure achievements and because each generation benefits from the efforts of the past and works for the good of the next, the question "For whom exactly does it pay?" cannot be answered.

This is how we wish to interpret the fact that in social life general intentions and slogans must be out of proportion to results so as to be in proportion to the sum of energy required. All projects for social reconstruction share this fate, especially in their moral content. Although, as our first assumption points out, no social system or institution is subject to moral appraisal because it is anonymous and impersonal, still the attitude of the individual toward it can be, and most often is, essentially moral, that is, subject to moral judgment in the general sense. There is no inconsistency in this statement. As our early example points out, a person who jumps into a river to save a drowning man is subject to moral appraisal, though the river is not. Therefore, when we decide to oppose or support a given social system—which from a moral point of view is itself indifferent—we become morally engaged, expose ourselves to moral judgment, and usually act out of moral motives. (We must note that we can use metaphor, that irradiation of meaning which the Thomists call *analogia attributionis*, wherein we transfer a certain property to an object that in itself does not possess it but that, for example, contributes to producing it in others—as when we say that whiskey is unhealthy, meaning that those who drink it are unhealthy. Just so a social system can induce human behavior that we find reprehensible and in this metaphorical sense we can call it "immoral.")

We formulate this thought as our:

SIXTH ASSUMPTION: *the possibility of ethical judgment of political choices. The fundamental political choices we make are subject to moral judgment.*

A world whose every element has been assigned a political allegiance, and in which total war is waged between political parties, produces a profound change in life. Our assumption, in fact, rejects the view that group solidarity is subject to moral judgment, whereas the fact itself of opting freely for one group rather than another is not. Since social life has become more intensely political than ever before, a tremendous number of our actions, which once passed as amoral, have taken on a moral coloration. That is why a shadow of anxiety trails behind daily life, even in its most trifling manifestations, for all of them are imbued with a tormenting awareness of their connnection with basic political conflicts. This universal system of interconnections between social actions has become an undeniable fact, regardless of what one thinks of its origins and of whether one approves or not. It is certainly possible to be regarded as a "decent man." But how many ways there are of being "decent"! And how many of them depend on the situation in which one finds oneself, independent of one's will!

What did it mean to be a "decent man" in Hitler Germany as a member of the super race? What does it mean to be a "decent man" and a member of a social-democratic party carrying out a policy of colonial terrorism? Who is "decent" in time of war? Or during elections? Yet in all these situations a "decent man" really does exist, and we have no reason to give up this category. True, it is misty and ill-defined, but still useful within limits.

It appears that political choices have assumed a total character. We merely state that this is so; we do not say it delights us. Within the framework of these total divisions, we have become aware of ties that link everyday life to the great events of history.

From the moment political choices cease to impose themselves with that unequivocalness which so simplifies life, this becomes an unhappy awareness. One may call this situation madness, but in the words of Pascal, "Men are so inevitably mad that not to be mad would mean to be mad with some different kind of madness." The awareness of participation in great conflicts, coupled with uncertainty about their outcome, has become a torment that is man's constant companion. This uncertainty does not consist of doubting victory—that is not morally appalling—but of not knowing to what extent the results of the great causes we are entangled in and partly responsible for will be morally acceptable tomorrow, or for that matter today. It is not true—though currently this is sometimes used to solve the crimes of a system—that it is enough to be a "decent man" in the trivial sense of the word, either in order to escape responsibility or to fulfill it faultlessly.

To voice such a principle is but to declare one's disbelief in the possibility of making rational political choices. This disbelief is substantiated by experience, but the fact is, we make these choices in so many small actions that avoiding them would be much more difficult than making them consciously. Machiavelli, in his famous dissertation on the first decade of Livy, observes that "People who often err as to the general results of an undertaking are less likely to err in regard to some particular fact." This idea would console us if we actually had to deal exclusively with individual facts which were tangible and easily evaluated. Instead, the voice of God pursues us within the four walls of our room, and the air we breathe is polluted with the dust of wars waged on Olympus. If someone in this situation seeks solace in the conviction that he can save his soul through personal decency "and the rest will take care of itself," then he is doomed to bitter disappointment when, on the other side of the Styx, they present him with a bill for crimes he knew nothing about. The whole tragedy lies in the fact that we are compelled to make morally binding decisions in total ignorance of their consequences.

Indeed, and this point should be stressed, ignorance does not absolve one of responsibility, because there are situations in which it is our moral duty to know. There were, it is true, Germans who did not know about the concentration camps. Who, if not they, is responsible for their ignorance? How could they be "decent people" if they took advantage—if only on the basis of their citizenship—of belonging to a nation that ruled half of Europe? We can say they were all the more guilty of ignorance because it was not difficult to overcome; and they were guilty in the general sense of unwillingness to acquaint themselves with their situation. But this is not enough. There are cases where it is not within our practical means to gain the knowledge required for a decision; yet once taken, it may entail unexpected results for which we feel responsible.

One may say that moral judgments pertain to intentions, not to the effects of our actions, and that "objective guilt"—a favorite category of political Stalinism—is a self-contradictory concept. We do not agree with this attitude because it lacks instruments of practical control over human responsibility. Of all the railroad accidents that happen in the world, how many are brought about by "intention"? Still, in almost all of them someone is held responsible. And it is not true that he is responsible only for neglecting his duty, not for the crash and its consequences. Derelictions of duties accepted as part of a job happen every day and everywhere; they differ only insignificantly and, more important, they certainly cannot be measurably differentiated by intentions. They can be compared only in the area of results, whose dimensions determine the guilt. If anyone finds this system of social responsibility irrational, he should note that no other concretely applicable system has yet been devised. All he can do is beg Jove for a better kind of world. (We do not mean to say, obviously, that intention is not a pertinent and necessary element in evaluation; we simply think it cannot be the exclusive basis for determining responsibility.) If everything we are responsible for grew out of intentions, and if our intentions were always ascertainable even by ourselves, then life would be as simple as Esperanto grammar. But such simplicity can be attained only by languages nobody speaks.

The conclusions that emerge from these assumptions can be formulated as follows:

To oppose existing social relations with a program based on moral postulates is not in itself socially useless, much less harmful. This is true even when the concrete realization of this program is highly problematical, if one weighs the potentials objectively inherent in that complex of relations. If the confrontation between "duty" and "existence" reveals an inordinately radical opposition and an enormous distance between them, then social life will automatically condemn these purely moralistic programs to sterility, preventing them from becoming a real force in a given human community. Therefore, according to the law of transposition, whenever such programs appear as a vital element in the social consciousness, whenever they are felt as a factor that noticeably influences public opinion, they prove thereby that they are not utopian, in the traditional meaning of the expression, and demonstrate by their partial effectiveness that they answer some actual social need.

Obviously this does not mean that they thereby become "real" in the sense that there is a possibility of their being speedily realized in a pure form. If the slogans that shape the collective consciousness appeal to moral feelings that are popular in a given period, they must, as we have said, necessarily reach far beyond the possibilities of the existing world—without, however, becoming disqualified as mere chimerical fancies. Throughout modern history the abstract, moralistic slogan of freedom has served as a battle cry for innumerable social movements. Of course it was never realized in that abstract, moralistic form. Nonetheless, many stages of a partial and fragmentary realization did indeed occur, and it would be stupid to disregard this catchword merely because its implementation was incomplete and did not fulfill maximal demands. (I exclude the fact that this slogan, like others, has its own deceptive and backward forms; they are, however, easily recognizable.) Let us stress once again that partial realization can take place only when the postulates exceed the actual "potentials" of reality. For only then are they able to organize and accumulate sufficient collective energy to achieve real progress. The disproportion between intention and possibility has a certain almost indefinable optimum, beyond which the accusation of utopianism becomes valid. Programs that advocate change but are too remote from possibility are condemned to impotence. Yet disproportions are necessary and for that reason characterize all the undertakings of left-wing social movements. *The excess of hopes and demands over possibilities is necessary in order to force reality to yield all the potentials it contains, and to tap all the resources hidden in it.*

True, overoptimism runs the risk of disappointment. It is also true that disappointment discourages further efforts and precludes organization of the social energy needed to exploit actual possibilities. This, in turn, brings about a decrease in the intensity of collective activity to a level below the potential. But disappointment is always a natural concomitant of the fulfillment of all intentions, individual and collective. That is why the collective consciousness oscillates continuously—now rising, now falling—between two points equally inadequate to the exploitation of the real potentials in the situation. These two points characterize two phases of the eternal consequences of each stage of social change. Illusions are indispensable if the non-illusory possibilities are to be realized; and when illusions are confronted with results disillusion is inevitable. The disillusions then slow down the exploitation of further nonillusory potentials. Between the appearance of the illusion and the setting in of disillusion, there is a lapse of time during which the slow, painful, burdensome labor of social progress takes place. For disillusions like illusions are not eternal; they yield eventually to the next illusions, certainly more advanced in their demands, but also somewhat richer to begin with. No one can foresee the duration of these cycles under different conditions. If its second half—from decline to rise—lasts the time of a generation, then that generation has the feeling of having wasted its life. This feeling is doubtless unjustified from the point of view of the philosophy of history, but it cannot be overcome.

The next conclusion to be drawn from our assumptions is: *Let us not underestimate the positive role of hypocrisy.* A social system based on lawlessness, constraint, and misery does not, all appearances to the contrary, become more effective in the long run by hiding behind a front of humanistic phraseology. At a given moment, this façade turns against the social system, because it was always alien and was imposed only by force of historical circumstances. *Generally speaking, the growth of hypocrisy is proof of moral progress,* for it indicates that what used to be done openly and without fear of censure can no longer be done without incurring that risk. That is to say, the moral consciousness of society has become more sensitive to stimuli to which it did not react previously. People are tortured as efficiently in the twentieth as in the fifteenth century, but it doesn't happen in public; and the fact that no government wishes to confess to the use of torture testifies that the moral feelings of society do not tolerate these procedures as a system. Military aggression continues, but everybody is well supplied with slogans condemning it; and the fact that no one wants to be called an aggressor proves that the idea of nonaggression as a positive principle has taken root in the public life. Whereas Mussolini was not afraid to avow that his was a policy of conquest, no politician today will admit to anything but self-defense. When the principle of self-determination of nations was first advocated by Lenin and the Bolshevik Party before the First World War, it was a novelty. After the Second World War it was recognized by the United Nations, and thus by governments engaged in the most infamous colonial oppression. The Nazis proclaimed the subjugation of other countries as the right of a superior nation; today one can offer nations only liberation, freedom, the progress of civilization.

We repeat that this false front of humanist phraseology, which covers even criminal systems, is not merely the product and the proof of a certain progress in social consciousness, but is in itself a positive factor that makes for progress. This façade sometimes begins to live a life of its own, and when it contradicts a system, it produces and nourishes the seeds of the destruction of the system. When an excessive attachment to tradition prevents the system from throwing off this deceptive attire, it may become a Deianira's shirt. The opposition between the façade and the content of the system is transformed into an internal contradiction of the system itself whenever the façade becomes alienated from the content—which is a natural turn of human events. The Marranos who, under compulsion, accepted the cult of an alien God, but who hid the books of the Talmud and worshiped Jehovah in their cellars, took the risk that their children would become true Christians and denounce their own parents to the Holy Office. That is why every social system that assumes a false front cannot help but enter into a pact with the devil, who some day will claim his due.

The general point of our discussion is therefore that rules of moral behavior cannot be derived from any theory of historical progress, and that no such theory can justifiably be used as a pretext for the violation of certain rules of whose validity we are otherwise convinced. In addition to the reasons presented above, there are two easily observable circumstances that support our conclusion: the very concept of progress has the nature of a value judgment; and there exists no theory of progress which is not inconsistent, which does not lead, on concrete application, to a conflict among various values each of which fulfills certain criteria and simultaneously excludes the others. Moral rules cannot have their source in a theory of an essentially moral progress because this concept, already burdened with all the shortcoming and difficulties of the general idea of progress, has additional flaws and problems of its own which make the formulation of a rational notion of progress seem a hopeless task. Actually, an investigation which uses value criteria to assess any moral evolution of society shows very clearly that the investigation does not so much alter and distort the object of study, as create it. But we have no other means of evaluating the past except our own criteria, formed under the influence of contemporary opinions, ideas, and prejudices. Consequently the question of whether or not there is moral progress is always a question of the extent to which history has carried out our personal preferences in the domain of morality, and of whether our opinions on these matters have gradually spread in society. One must expect an affirmative answer if one formulates the question thus. Since I and my opinions are products of history, I will observe that the set of values I myself profess is more widely recognized today than before, if only because I have accepted it precisely because of its popularity. The question is meaningless.

However, our opposition to a certain moral Hegelianism, or rather pseudo-Hegelianism, does not lead to the conviction that our moral views can be—even though only in our own minds— independent of our knowledge of society. (This is not a matter of causal dependence, which is universal, regardless of the degree to which we are conscious of it. Our values are always a product of history and society. It is a question of knowing how far we must personally take into account certain needs of the historical processes in which we are entangled in considering the moral decisions we are forced to make.)

Only the vaguest observations can be formulated in this matter. The main values we accept are really, according to our third assumption, unprovable in the strict sense of the word. This means that, in case of conflict between two evaluations, if there is not a possibility of appeal to some more general common values, discussion becomes impossible. This is not an alarming situation. As our second assumption states, since values are the product of history, in practice there always exists a certain sum of very general, universally accepted values to which we can appeal. The real difficulty lies in the permanent conflicts among unquestioned values when they are applied concretely; we are often incapable of settling these. Since, in line with our sixth assumption, our basic political choices have moral aspects, they must appear to the individual consciousness as somewhat risky, for we assume that the values we recognize have the greatest probability of being embodied in a specific and limited form of existing social activity.

This risk pertains to a judgment of facts, not of values. It is a kind of stake that one wagers on the probability of the realization of values. The stake is always huge and always morally binding, for it brings with it responsibility for the unforeseeable consequences of the bet. Still, since the risk hinges on a certain judgment of facts, or of historical processes which have to take place in fact, we have at least one permanent duty: to re-examine our choice incessantly by investigating all the facts related to it, and to be constantly, vigilantly aware that our choice always concerns probabilities, not certainties, and therefore can always be put in question or demolished by facts. The values we have espoused can never justify a lack of knowledge of the actual results of the social action we have undertaken. We are not absolved of neglect, laziness, or sleepy indolence in respect to the need for ceaseless verification of our choice; our ignorance is not condoned if it leads us to conform to crime. The borderline between innocent ignorance and deliberate blindness cannot be drawn; in the last anaylsis, we are responsible for both. Each choice we make arises from a combination of the values we affirm (for which we are held to account by society, though the act of affirmation itself does not depend on us) and of knowledge about the probabilities of their being realized in specific conditions. This being so, our knowledge must be the subject of constant, most suspicious and most pitiless control, allowing for everything which can prove it false. We are obliged to know everything that argues against us. Each of our choices contains a risk, and none can pretend to be final and irrevocable simply on the grounds that it is being fulfilled.

Even the greatest errors are not excluded. Furthermore, not even the most dangerous conflicts among professed values are excluded either. No moral doctrine can remove such conflicts, and none can be free of contradictions in its application. Thus we are powerless before the inevitable appearance of a situation in which no one is guilty from the point of view of naked intentions, but all are morally responsible. In other words, tragedies are a permanent possibility of the world we live in. When we oppose skepticism to bigotry masked as faith, when we oppose the principle of responsibility to that of conformism disguised as theoretical relativism, when we oppose the duty of individual choice to an opportunistic philosophy of history masquerading as realism, when we oppose rationalism to a superstitious cult of unverified "laws of history," when we oppose the principle of active engagement to the principle of humility and obedience —when we set up these antitheses, we do not intend to regard them as solutions to the actual conflicts that we fall into when we invoke our accepted general rules of moral behavior. If these situations originate in the contradictory nature of social reality, they are solved at a risk that is no longer theoretical but moral, and that each man takes upon himself.

I realize that these questions have a limited social vitality, at least in the form presented here. In this limited sphere they nevertheless reflect some very general conflicts that are constantly active in disguised shapes and that are as explosive as dynamite at important moments of history: the conflict between the social feeling of justice and the social sense of necessity; between political exigencies and actual possibilities: the conflict between "duty" (*Sollen*) and "existence" (*Sein*) in all its manifestations.

The inevitability of what exists is the inevitability of the past, for all that actually exists is the past. The idea of the inevitability of the past is tautological and arouses no controversy. The inevitability of what does not yet exist is doubtful; to establish what it consists of is as chancy as roulette, and in any case the part our decisions play is difficult to determine. Because prophetic historiosophy proves its poverty daily, the decisions for which we bear moral responsibility cannot be based on faith in its prognostications. A philosophy of history worthy of respect describes only what has already in some manner come into existence —that is, only the past, not the future creations of the historical process. Therefore, those who attempt to justify through history's indications their own involvement in predicted processes are like tourists who scribble their names on the walls of dead cities. Everyone can if he wishes interpret himself historically and unearth the determining factors that made him what he is—his past—but he cannot do the same for the self he has not yet become. He cannot, trusting the verdicts of historiosophy, infer from his past his own future transformations. To perform this miracle would mean to become the past itself, in other words to cross the river of death, which, says the poet, no man may look at twice.

Intellectuals and the Communist Movement

If we use the word intelligentsia to mean the sum total of educated people as well as those who earn their living by mental work or at least consider that their main occupation, then we can readily observe that this group has been indispensable to the functioning of the state almost from the moment it first appeared in history. Its clear differentiation in modern capitalist countries is due to two circumstances. First, in a capitalist society the majority of educated people actually earn their living from intellectual pursuits and not, as they did in antiquity, for example, from simultaneous ownership of the means of production. Second, the role of education, learning, cultural life, and intellectual refinement has grown immeasurably in modern times —particularly where government is increasingly democratic. Aside from the fact that it is impossible to live in contemporary society without doctors and engineers, and that a great number of specialists are needed to organize the apparatus of government and the courts, the intelligentsia is the group that is involved with most of the intellectual media and that has the skill to educate and influence culturally.

On the other hand, it does not as a body control (at least to any appreciable degree) the material and technical conditions of this influence, and thus easily becomes dependent on groups that are either economically stronger or that rule the state. The degree of dependence and also the strength of the ties that bind the intelligentsia to the political order in which it lives vary with each stratum. It is obvious, for example, that in capitalist countries civil servants, for whom the maintenance of government represents a guarantee of a lifetime job, must be more conservative than the artists.

In speaking of intellectuals from here on, I have in mind only those who might be called the pedagogic intelligentsia, meaning not only the personnel of all levels of schools, but all those whose profession is to create and communicate cultural values—scientific information, an outlook on the world, works of art, knowledge of current society, political opinions—in short, scientists, teachers, artists, journalists, propagandists, and the like. In particular, however, we are concerned here with people professionally engaged in theoretical work in fields relating to the organization of the life of society. Now the spiritual dominion of any ruling class over the people, far more than its material domination, depends on its bonds with the intelligentsia. That is why those in power in all social orders strive to maintain the closest possible cooperation with the intellectuals. Failing this, they must rely exclusively on the support of the police and the army—apparently the most efficient method, yet experience has shown it to be deceptive if it is the sole means of ruling. The participation of the pedagogic intelligentsia in the system of government is, other things being equal, in inverse proportion to the degree of repression; for the less one is capable of ruling by intellectual means, the more one must resort to the instruments of force. That is why intellectuals so often attract the instinctive animosity of the police and the army.

It is also a natural phenomenon that while the economic war of the working class could be born spontaneously without the cooperation of the educated milieux, an organized communist movement was inconceivable without the participation of people who belonged to the bourgeois intelligentsia but were able to evaluate the future prospects of the proletariat and to assume a role in life compatible with its natural historical tendency.

The theory of scientific socialism could not be the automatic result of class conflict; it could not be the product of "class instinct" nor the creation of the workers themselves. It required the mastery of all existing knowledge about society, attainable only after prolonged specialized study. Hence, as Lenin said, the necessity to bring socialist ideology "from outside" into the working-class movement, which was itself incapable of producing it.

Hence also the far from accidental circumstance that the most famous leaders of the proletariat—Marx, Engels, Lenin—were intellectuals by education, origin, and nature of work. None of them could have played his political role without a multifaceted educational training which enabled him to analyze contemporary social life economically and politically and to understand the perspectives of its future transformations.

Theoretical knowledge of society continues to be a condition for the successful struggle of the communist movement. If this movement is not to stagnate, it must still be nourished by advances in theory, created and nurtured by communist intellectuals. The role of the intellectuals in the communist movement is thus, and always has been, incomparably greater than in laborite parties, which are concerned almost exclusively with immediate economic gains and devoid of more long-range objectives in the proletariat's fight for power, or of plans for the organization of economic life within this framework. On the other hand, a movement that sets itself political goals, that seeks to break the bourgeois hold on the reins of state and to rebuild completely all areas of human life, cannot do without a theory that is constantly subjected to criticism, modernization, and revision. Only thus can the theory remain on a level that corresponds to the actual situation and to current social changes in the world. Intellectuals who create the theoretical foundations of political action are, therefore, not merely "helpers" in the workers' movement, but an indispensable condition for its existence.

Their role in this movement is clearly evident in the impasse that now exists in Marxist theory. The reconstruction of a Marxism adequate to the needs of this era—the era of the atom bomb, of imperialism in its current phase, of contemporary bourgeois culture, and of the existence of a socialist camp made up of various states—is a task which may have a decisive influence on the future of communism. It is clear, for example, that the resolution of the question whether the so-called law of "absolute impoverishment" is applicable in today's capitalistic world must have an actual influence on the policy of the entire labor movement. This question cannot be turned away with a phrase or with sophistry. It demands special scientific study and discussion limited by nothing other than the search to ascertain the objective state of things. This also holds true for the relationship of the Marxist theory of crisis to modern capitalism; and for the theory of socialist revolution, in which practical instructions minus factual proof do not suffice. It also applies to the very theory of the Party and its role in a state it governs, particularly in regard to the correctness of the view that the basic duty of Party organizations is to supervise the smooth operation of the production apparatus and to act as an inspectorate in manufacturing establishments. Similarly, it is valid for all the problems connected with the mechanism of power in all lands ruled by the Communist Party, as well as for the relationship of political life to new social and economic stratifications and the new social hierarchies arising within them.

Without such analyses, conducted in absolute freedom and requiring, among other things, a rebirth of sociology as an independent science instead of a collection of popular banalities—without these, the Party cannot know or foresee the real consequences of its own decisions. Then such hazards arise as the naïve and dangerous, though extremely idealistic, belief in the possibility of replacing economic laws by the influence of ideology, or in the need to increase repressive measures as a result of incapacity to manage technology. One thing is certain, however: the less we succeed in managing things, the more we are forced to administer people. It then becomes possible for good intentions to turn into their opposites, and for ignorance of the dependencies of social life to yield unexpected consequences.

However, the role of the intelligentsia in the communist movement is not limited to its indispensable theoretical work in the domain of politics. Intellectuals are the actual creators of socialist culture in its most diverse forms, but above all in intellectual and artistic aspects. This means that they give expression to those tendencies of historical evolution that lead to the destruction of capitalism and that are brought about as a result of the struggle of the exploited classes. This expression is pertinent to the social current and is capable of influencing the shape of social consciousness.

In capitalist conditions of life, the proletariat necessarily remains under the constant cultural pressure of those groups with which it is in closest contact and between which the most common crossing from one class to another takes place: the peasantry and the lower middle class. Without the help of the intelligentsia it is difficult for the workers to free themselves from the cultural influence of the lower middle class. (Just so, the intelligentsia, by virtue of another social mechanism, could never conquer its spiritual dependence on capitalism without binding itself to the destiny of the working class.) Even the spiritual life of the new society threatens to be inundated by peasant tastes and habits which could stifle socialist culture. As we know, twentieth-century avant-garde arts (painting, poetry, literature, theater) in their beginnings had chiefly, though obviously not entirely, a clearly leftist orientation. This was true of futurism, expressionism, and cubism. ("Cubism—bolshevik art," Hitler wrote in *Mein Kampf.*) Quite possibly, one of these trends that the official doctrine so brutally repudiated bore the seeds of a future culture. The same can be said of many new developments in different realms of science.

This, of course, does not mean that the workers can be only the passive object of cultural creation that takes place independently of them. It is clear that their fight and their situation are necessary conditions for the rise of a social culture whose chief elements, especially those of morality, are formed spontaneously in the process of class struggle. Nevertheless, the working class, especially in agricultural countries, cannot successfully withstand the overwhelming pressure of petit-bourgeois culture and customs. And at the current level of cultural life, art, a very influential social tool, cannot in fact develop without the education of what is often an extremely exclusive group, and cannot reach a high standard except among the intellectuals.

If it is true that the economic and political life of a communist-ruled country and the life of the Party itself are dependent on scientific and cultural creativity, then it is also true that that creativity is even more dependent upon how the political power of the state is exercised. Cultural phenomena are the most sensitized tissues of the social organism and therefore feel most keenly the destructive radiation of foci of degeneration when they appear in that organism. It is natural that the sum of events conventionally and symbolically referred to as "the cult of the individual," as well as all the elements of rule by one person or by an oligarchy, spread their corrupt and restrictive influence even to intellectual life. The continuing violation of democracy—that is, of the principle of the broadest possible participation of popular opinion in important decisions that affect collective life (the principle which essentially differentiates the revolutionary movement from a religious sect)—led to inertia in mass initiative and paralyzed external possibilities and, in time, also individual and collective creative abilities that might have been used in economic, political, and intellectual life.

Religion is the death of science. Over a long period of time, religion also became the actual form of cultural life of many intellectual circles—religion with all its accessories: the intrusion of revelation into the field of cognition, a system of magic and tabus, a priestly caste monopolizing the right to proclaim the truth, the ideology's endeavor to absorb totally all forms of human life (intellectual pursuits, art, customs, etc.). It is not true that this state of affairs followed inexorably once Marxism took on a mass character. Bruno Bauer's contention that any theory changes into a religion as soon as it is shared by the masses is false. Quite the contrary. One of the main reasons why this situation arose was the monopolizing of theoretical creative thought. As a result, an utter contempt for theory came to be voiced under the guise of declarations about its great worth. In fact, theory worked ex post facto, fashioning reasons for previously made decisions; it neither changed the world nor enlightened it. Forced to justify the most divergent moves, it necessarily became fuzzy; and the dialectic—an incisive tool for analyzing social phenomena in their full dynamics of evolution and internal conflict—was equated with ambiguity and lack of precision.

Once theory was reduced to an instrument of apology and its

intellectual function sterilized, that situation became inevitable. It was said that "on the one hand" the masses create history, and "on the other hand" an individual who understands the trends of history can influence its course, and so forth. This statement is so nebulous that it can both justify and attack the deification of an autocrat. "On the one hand" one should overcome nationalism, and one should combat cosmopolitanism "on the other hand"; on the basis of such generalities one can easily tolerate chauvinistic escapades now, then condemn them loudly as the need arises. The examples are innumerable. An all-purpose theory based on such vague formulations as "yes and no" or "on the one hand and on the other" had to defend itself scrupulously against any precision, for its strength lay in its blurriness. This was the consequence of, among other things, the popular understanding of the principle of the class nature of social theories. Primitive pseudo-Marxist sociology held that the entire content of these theories was determined by class interests. (In view of this, the multiplicity of trends in bourgeois sociology and philosophy was quite puzzling.) It follows that the entire content of Marxist doctrine is determined by the interests of the working-class party. And since these interests, as another postulate has it, cannot conflict with the growth of true knowledge of the world, then everything that serves these interests is true. However, precisely what serves these interests was defined without theory and only by political decisions. Under these conditions, theory had to act on the principle that everything that is real is reasonable—an utterly trivial interpretation.

"Order" was introduced into the theory in the sense that it was brought into an apparently systematized whole; but in fact it became a hermetically sealed, exhaustive compilation of possible theoretical problems and a whole stock of permissible fetishistic concepts inaccessible to analysis. The principle on which this straightening up is introduced doesn't matter. In the end it is all the same whether one teaches Marxism according to the four "sins" of the dialectic or according to scores of "categories," so long as one tacitly postulates that they constitute the total apparatus of concepts permitted in use and are imposed as the sole and obligatory system of organizing one's thinking. Every petrification of doctrine leads necessarily to its transformation into a mythology, an object of worship, surrounded by a ritualistic cult and immune to criticism. In this situation theoretical progress becomes impossible; and new dogmas that appear are monopolized and served up, with no reasons given, as articles of faith. At such times shameful banalities are promulgated as theoretical accomplishments. The explanation that not all technological discoveries are the work of a single nation seems like a painful joke; and the truth that all phenomena in the world influence each other mutually passes as the formulation of genius—yet it is a commonplace found in scores of very diverse philosophical trends over the centuries. Ancient truisms are presented as the creative results of scientific progress. It is deeply degrading to have to state that one should not falsify historical documents, that in science the opinions one expresses must be substantiated, that criticism of one's scientific opponent must be material, and so on.

In the present condition of Marxist theory one might well wish Karl Marx could be resurrected. But since that is highly unlikely, the theoretical work that is supposed to create for the communist movement a scientific basis for political activity adequate to the needs of our times can be only a collective effort on the part of communist intellectuals who are trained in various fields of knowledge about society, and who are capable of utilizing the everyday experiences of the masses and are attuned to the voice of public opinion. This is also necessary if the communist world outlook is to be able to react to the cultural problems of our day. Just as there is a great deal of money in circulation outside the control of state banks and official statistics, so there is a cultural life pulsing beneath the slogans on our banners.

Communist intellectuals have the responsibility to fight for the secularization of thinking, to combat pseudo-Marxist mythology and bigotry as well as religio-magic practices, and to struggle to rebuild respect for completely unrestricted secular reason. Daily experience teaches us that this process is not ended and cannot run its course without great opposition from a large number of people (and also organizations and institutions) whose social position is supported solely by an antidemocratic method of wielding power and by a closely related anti-intellectualism. Since, as we have said, overcoming the tendency to make a fetish of the theory is in itself a condition for effective political activity on the part of the communist movement, the participation of intellectuals opposed to all mythology constitutes an indispensable prerequisite to all efforts aimed at a political rebirth of the Party. The creative circles of the intelligentsia, because of their professions, are particularly sensitive to impulses of modernity in the most varied realms of life, and can most easily rid themselves of conservativism.

In order for the intelligentsia, and especially scientific circles, to fulfill their normal function, as defined by the social division of labor, we must remove the limitations that have arisen in this period as a result of the misconception of the relationship between science and politics and the wrong methods used to resolve the conflicts between them.

First of all, any political restriction on the subject matter of scientific research is damaging. Yet it continues to exist. Consequently, when one realizes that the results of one's analysis in a given field can be neither published nor used, it is hard to make the analysis the subject of a collective research project. (This applies particularly to certain segments of political history and to the history of the ideology, as well as to certain questions regarding contemporary life in the countries that have been emancipated from capitalism.)

Second, it is equally harmful, in a field that is still subject to scientific research, to announce that certain truths are "politically correct" and to demand that they be disseminated without regard to scientific discussion. Whenever this is the practice, humanistic sciences are moribund and their work amounts to no more than placing garlands on the plaster of Paris façades of socialist life— which is done sincerely by those who are less discerning, and cynically by the more intelligent. Scientific cynicism is the natural product of the rape of the principles of scientific thought.

Third, to lay down certain *directions for research* in scientific circles (while indispensable in domains closely related to technology) is dangerous in humanistic studies because it often conceals a demand that they supply arguments for views accepted beforehand as being correct. This becomes a process of imposing theses under the guise of posing questions. (We do not lack examples of such operations.) It is far better, in this respect, to trust the collective competence of communist intellectuals.

Fourth, it is both dangerous and irresponsible to establish a sphere of untouchable truths that are excluded from discussion. This means that nonscientific points of view have a monopoly of science, since bodies with authority over this sphere must exist. Such exclusions are impossible, if only because the basic concepts in humanistic studies, especially sociology and philosophy, generally have manifold meanings, and consequently so do the theses that involve these concepts. To predetermine the boundaries of permissible discussion threatens to make the words "Marxism" and "Marxist" tools of blackmail, and to replace scientific polemic with administrative pressure, which is a mask for theoretical weakness. Obviously this is not meant to advocate unrestricted freedom for all the forms of antiscience which never seem to lack nourishment in our intellectual life, but merely to create an atmosphere in which scientific factors—which can be determined by creative professional groups—will set the limits of discussion. Wherever there exists a catalogue of propositions outside discussion, somewhat like scholastic dogmatism, there thinking becomes apologetics. This sequence is only too well proved in the history of culture and anticulture.

All these rules pertain, however, to only one element in the situation: influence on scientific milieux that ignores their opinions and is contrary to the principles of their work. The second element is the matter of the social responsibility of these groups. For communists working scientifically on questions of sociology or philosophy do not cease to be communists. And the workers' movement does not have only political goals, but also its own concept of the world, which includes many scientific theses. It seems, therefore, that the communist as such is duty-bound to accept a certain number of postulates of a scientific nature and at the same time, if he wants to maintain a scientific attitude, he must be convinced that there are no assertions which are a *priori* exempt from criticism, discussion, or revision. This constitutes the main difference between science and theology. It is impossible to hold that the workers' movement does not possess its own outlook on the world, and equally impossible to regard certain truths as untouchable. There exists now a clearly recognized need to attack the degenerate, cancerous growth of the ideology which led to the belief that the Party must profess certain dicta on the laws of biological heredity or the best forms of musical expression. While the catastrophic consequences of such a system are obvious, it is equally obvious that to reduce communist ideology to political goals unrelated to a scientific foundation would be just as disastrous. It is also unquestionably true that an educated humanist is not a purely intellectual being motivated solely by a desire to know, but a person subject to diverse social influences and not independent of the determinism of a class, group, or clan. We cannot ignore this fact.

Without postulating the fiction of a learned man who is solely erudite—a distilled intellect motivated exclusively by scientific reasoning—we can avoid the contradictions in the situation described above if we seriously accept, and not just pay lip service to, the principle that the interests of the communist movement are not at variance with an objective knowledge of the world, that is, that the *political* inspiration of this movement, whose intellectual genealogy is the entire tradition of European rationalism, cannot lead to the deformation of scientific truth for the purpose of proving "truths" settled beforehand or served up for belief. In other words, scientific activity led by the real interests of communism depends on the maximum amount of freedom from all nonscientific motivation in establishing the content of knowledge and on the formation of the most resolutely objective and critical attitude. Given this, there is no need for a catalogue of holy principles. In scientific work essential to the workers' movement, no other criteria are necessary than those generally observed and created by science. There is no contradiction between the desire for objective scientific knowledge and the fight for the political objectives of the movement. The party's ideology in the realm of sociological, economic, and philosophical questions must be worked out by the people who are most competent and must be controlled by the collective experience of society. Communist intellectuals have the obligation, as well as the right, to bear the responsibility for the ideological development of the revolutionary movement. On the other hand, they have neither the right nor the duty to accept, for this purpose, any *a priori* principles as being inaccessible to control and discussion.

Because the opposite has been the practice for years, one of the most important tasks presently facing Marxist scientists is to return to and perpetuate in intellectual activity the rules which apply to *all* theoretical work as well as the general principles of rational thought and the highest scientific *techniques*.

No one has ever yet won a war simply because he was defending the right cause; and in scientific life, technical skill is of decisive importance. As Machiavelli so justly remarked, all armed prophets have been victorious and all unarmed ones have suffered defeat. Lasting and practically useful scientific discoveries result from high technical competence. Attaining that level of competence is for the moment more important than setting subjects for research. (Needless to add, the elementary condition for progress in this field is to create free time for scientists; nowadays inspired improvisations rarely occur in science.) We have no reason to suppose that rational thought operating on the basis of sound technique forces the scientist to come into conflict with the objectives of the workers' movement, for whose future he is jointly responsible.

Unfortunately there is a certain amount of fiction in this reasoning, namely the belief that rational thinking, free of prejudices and foregone conclusions, can be disseminated to such a degree that everyone who accepts Marxism will do so on the basis of independent scientific analysis. This is false. Marxist ideology, particularly in its most specialized aspects, is undoubtedly effective on a broad social scale even when it takes the paths of faith. Just as the legal fiction of political economics that Marx wrote about posited that all merchants have an encyclopedic knowledge of products, so we tacitly assume that dealers in world outlooks are guided solely by rational motives. But if this is not so, then are we allowed to maintain the above postulates? We can certainly resist the pressures of pseudo-Marxist irrationalism on science. We can liberate cultural life from nonscientific influences on the ascertainment of what is true; combat falsifications and lies; liquidate toleration of lack of knowledge and absence of criticism; and prevent the subjugation of theory to current tactical considerations. In a word, we must remove the causes which led to a situation in which the so-called ideological disciplines have lost their social credit, and fight to restore an intellectually grounded confidence to them.

But communist intellectuals must then agree to propagate Marxism on a mass scale, one in which purely scientific motivations are not enough. Can certain *scientific* truths be taken on *faith* when one cannot in practice demand that they be accepted on scientific bases? Obviously they can—in accordance with general practice in all other areas of knowledge, where certain conclusions are presented to nonspecialists without explanation. There is nothing shocking in this. What matters is to perform this duty as a popularization of science, that is, to communicate knowledge of the world as scientific knowledge and not as "politically correct" truths. One need not imagine that because Marxism is a scientific theory it can or must be accepted by all its adherents on scientific grounds. Such a supposition does not raise popularization to the level of science; on the contrary, it transforms all science into popularization. (The latter was the official program of, for example, those who opposed starting a philosophical journal in the Soviet Union, arguing that the Party press sufficed as a tribune for all work in this field.)

Faith that is fostered by the growth of knowledge about society is different from faith based on natural science. A nonspecialist believes in the formula that mass depends on velocity differently from the way he believes that the dynamic of social processes depends more on class conflicts than on any other aspect of human relations. The latter belief finds various forms of substantiation in daily life and therefore is not accepted merely on the strength of scientific authority. Nevertheless, it cannot really be proved without a thorough knowledge of history and economics. The experiences of daily life are not sufficient proof.

On the other hand, there must be a conviction in the field of intellectual creativity that everything should be analyzed anew and subjected to doubt (which does not mean rejected). A scientist must not have an iota of pity for the subject of his research if he does not wish to plunge theoretical work deeper into the state from which it is just beginning to extricate itself with such difficulty. Nor can he ever excuse himself in any matter related to the subject of his studies—history, for example—on the grounds that he was deceived, for it is his duty not to let himself be deceived in his field of competence. This holds true for political life as well, and not merely in regard to scientists. To listen to lies in politics is no excuse; it is often as great a sin as to recount them.

A theory that for any reason falsifies reality becomes defenseless and loses the power to influence. And though panegyrics proclaim its great worth, it is like a maid of all work dressed in royal robes made of paper—an object of derision.

The Communist Party needs intellectuals not so that they can marvel at the wisdom of its decisions, but only so that its decisions will be wise. Intellectuals are necessary to communism as people who are free in their thinking, and superfluous as opportunists. Theoretical work cannot be useful to the revolutionary movement if it is controlled by anything besides scientific stringency and the striving for true knowledge; it must therefore be free for the good of the movement. That is why communist intellectuals who come to the defense of thought independent of political pressure do so not only in the name of an abstract freedom of knowledge, but also in the interests of communism, which, as we have known ever since the *Communist Manifesto*, has no interests—in regard to either production or culture—that are distinct from the interests of all humanity.

To make a fetish of Marxism, to reduce it to a conventional apologetic ornamentation that finds its place only on the façade of society, means that instead of being the lifeblood of intellectual life Marxism can become its poison. One should not for this reason belittle its creative capabilities. After all, even a precision instrument can be used to crush skulls. What we need for the development of Marxism is not "new formulations" that have to be learned by rote, but an objective and highly technical analysis of new, as well as old, social phenomena.

In order to achieve this end, one must have confidence in the Marxist self-knowledge of scientists and in the socialist consciousness of the intelligentsia. Without them it would be impossible to banish mythology from intellectual life, primitivism and backwardness from culture, blindness and irresponsibility from politics, obscurantism from customs, and all reaction—whatever its name —from human life.

Permanent vs. Transitory Aspects of Marxism

A few days after the Greatest Philologist in the World (Stalin) published in a daily newspaper his opus announcing that Marr's theory was false,[1] I had the opportunity to attend a congress of philologists on this very subject. In the course of the discussion one of the participants made a most tactless step. He produced a pamphlet issued several weeks earlier by one of his colleagues who was present and read an extract that ran roughly as follows: "It is quite obvious that in linguistics Marr's theory is the only genuine Marxist-Leninist theory of language, that it alone is compatible with the principles of Marxism-Leninism, that it is the sole infallible instrument of Marxist-Leninist research," etc. Then the malicious fellow produced the current issue of the daily newspaper and quoted sections from an article by the same author that said, more or less: "It is obvious that Marr's theory has nothing in common with Marxism-Leninism, that it is a striking vulgarization of Marxism-Leninism, that the Marxist-Leninist conception of language must be firmly opposed to Marr's theory," etc. "What is the meaning of this?" raged the critic. "Of such a change of view within a few weeks? What a chameleon!" Confounded, the author of the quoted passages remained silent while everyone laughed merrily, until a Party activist pointed out that they should not laugh because every man had a right to change his mind and this should not in itself be considered a disgrace.

As I listened, my first impression was that the critic had been right in showing up the opportunism of the philologist and his shameful readiness to reverse his opinions with lightning speed to conform to the judgment delivered by the Greatest Philologist in

1. N. J. Marr (1864–1934) was a Soviet linguist whose "japhetic theory" of languages was dogma in the Soviet Union until Stalin's pronouncement.—Trans.

the World. Only later, much later, did I realize that the embar-
rassed author of the pamphlet was the genuine Marxist, whereas
the critic had shown himself to be completely ignorant. Because—
and this is the core of the question I wish to consider—Marr's
theory was *truly* compatible with Marxism two days before the
publication of the Greatest Philologist's work, and *truly* incompatible with Marxism on the day this work appeared. Since the
author of the pamphlet was an authentic Marxist he had no
reason to be ashamed, but ought to have prided himself on his
unshakable faithfulness to the principles of Marxism.

Principles? Perhaps this is an awkward choice of words. The
point is that the term "Marxism" did not designate a doctrine
with a specific content. It meant a doctrine defined purely
formally, its content being in every case supplied by the decrees
of the Infallible Institution which, during a certain phase, was
the Greatest Philologist, the Greatest Economist, the Greatest
Philosopher, and the Greatest Historian in the World.

In short, "Marxism" became a concept of institutional, rather
than intellectual, content—which, by the way, happens to every
doctrine connected with a church. Similarly, the word "Marxist"
does not describe a man who believes in a specific world view
whose content is defined. It refers to a man with a mental attitude
characterized by a willingness to adopt institutionally approved
opinions. From this point of view, the current content of Marxism
does not matter. A man is a Marxist if he is always ready to accept
as its content each recommendation of the Office. This is why,
until February, 1956, the only real Marxist (which also means a
revolutionary, a dialectician, a materialist) was one who agreed
that there was no way to socialism except through revolutionary
violence. An anti-Marxist (that is, a reformer, a metaphysician,
an idealist) was anyone who thought other means could be found.
As we know, after February, 1956, the reverse became true: since
then the only real Marxist has been one who recognizes the possibility of a peaceful transition to socialism in certain countries.
It is difficult to predict accurately who will, in regard to this problem, be a Marxist next year. But we will not be the ones to decide
—the Office will settle the matter.

It is precisely for this reason, because of the institutional rather than the intellectual character of Marxism, that a true Marxist will profess beliefs he does not necessarily understand. The 1950 Marxist knew that Lysenko's theory of heredity was correct, that Hegel represented the aristocratic reaction to the French Revolution, that Dostoevski was a decadent and Babaevski a great writer, that Suvorov served the cause of progress, and also that the resonance theory in chemistry was reactionary nonsense. Every 1950 Marxist knew these things even if he had never heard of chromosomes, had no idea what century Hegel lived in, had never read one of Dostoevski's books or studied a high-school chemistry textbook. To a Marxist all this is absolutely unnecessary so long as the content of Marxism is determined by the Office.

In this way the concept of Marxism was defined very precisely, without any possibility of error, although the definition was purely formal; that is, it merely indicated where to look for the current content of Marxism, without actually specifying that content.

Chronologically, this appears to be the second concept of Marxism. The original one simply meant the sum total of views and theories characteristic of Karl Marx. This first, historical concept of Marxism still retains its validity and precision (in the same sense that the concepts of "Platonism," "Freudianism," and "Cartesianism" do) irrespective of whether any Marxist—meaning, in this context, a believer in Marx's views—exists in the world.

We are thus faced with a question: If the sort of Marxism in which doctrine was continuously established by the Office is now dead in the minds of most intellectuals who considered themselves Marxists, has the concept of Marxism retained any meaning at all? If so, what meaning, other than the historical one connected with the work of the man who gave his name to the doctrine? What sense is there in slogans urging the "development of Marxism," and what meaning remains in the division between Marxists and non-Marxists in science?

Before the Office was born, and with it a new concept of Marxism, the reply to this question was not very difficult. Outstanding theoreticians—Russian revolutionaries like Lenin, Trotsky, and Bukharin—when analyzing, for example, the social conditions and history of Russia, applied Marx's conceptual framework to situations Marx himself never considered. They used the Marxist concept of class—undoubtedly a theoretical novelty that distinguished Marxism from other doctrines—to describe the relations of forces in Russian society. Here it is clear what is meant by "development of Marxism": the application of Marx's method and conceptual apparatus to new subjects of study. Let us suppose, however, that certain social processes arise for which this conceptual apparatus is no longer adequate. We can admit the adequacy of this apparatus as applied to the capitalist societies so scrupulously analyzed by Marx, and also recognize the basic accuracy of such analyses, while at the same time maintaining that this conceptual scheme is not applicable to the study of new, noncapitalist societies, where new concepts must be used to study basic social stratification. (This problem, among others, is discussed by Stanislaw Ossowski in his still unpublished work *Concepts of Class Structure in the Social Consciousness*, which I had an opportunity to see in manuscript.) Can the attempt to build such a new apparatus aspire to be called "Marxist"? It is contradictory to Marxism, therefore "non-Marxist," if we assume that Marx's original conceptual categories are all that is necessary to describe and analyze every social phenomenon that might ever occur. Marx, of course, never made any such assumption; it is an original contribution of his Stalinist Epigoni. Yet if such an attempt is merely not contradictory to Marxism, does this mean that it becomes Marxist?

Obviously we might agree to call all the achievements of science and all scientific truths by the name of "Marxism," but then we would have to consider as Marxist all discoveries in astro-botany, every new physiological law, and every new proposition in topology. In this sense, which has sometimes been specifically postulated, the word "Marxism" is stripped of meaning and becomes a superfluous synonym for "truth" or "scientific knowledge." This synonym is not simply superfluous but also mystifying, because it deviously suggests that all human knowledge is either inspired by Karl Marx or else progresses only thanks to the method he formulated—which is obviously false.

And yet, to return to our example, if we wish to develop a new conceptual apparatus to analyze social stratification in types of societies unknown to Marx, we must fall back upon a certain methodological rule which he not only consistently observed but applied so forcefully and universally that it is typical of his work. According to this rule, all analyses of social life should proceed by seeking the basic divisions that separate societies into antagonistic groups. Even if it turns out that in certain societies these divisions are based on other criteria than the ones Marx formulated for the nineteenth-century bourgeois world, still the very fact of applying this extremely general rule leads the scholar to adopt Marx's characteristic methodology. From this point of view it can be said that the sociological research he is engaging in is "Marxist."

It happens, though, that the progress of knowledge requires us not only to enrich our supply of conceptual tools and methodological rules as compared with those found in Marx's works, but also to question and revise some of his concrete statements. The Office itself once proclaimed that some of Engels' assumptions about the origin of the state were false. In accordance with its usual procedures, it did not bother to justify this revision, but for the purposes of our discussion that is of secondary importance. Moreover, the Office disavowed Marx's thesis that it was impossible to build a socialist society in one isolated country. When Stalin came out with his concept of socialism in one country, Trotsky, as an orthodox and classical Marxist, rebuked him for deviating from the principles of Marxism and was, in turn, called an anti-Marxist by Stalin. Refraining for the moment from judging who was right in this dispute and whose view was verified by historical developments, we can nevertheless clearly see the scholastic sterility of a dispute conducted this way. If we say, as Stalin did, that the international situation has changed since Marx's time and that Marx himself recommended that the future of socialism be weighed in terms of the current structure of class power on an international scale, we are taking recourse to a way of thinking employed by Marx but so generalized and so common to all those who want to analyze reality rationally that it is not specifically symptomatic of "Marxist" thinking. On the other hand, if we maintain, as Lenin and Trotsky did, that Marx's analysis in this realm is not obsolete, we are falling back on the distinguishing features of Marx's method and on the concrete results of his analyses. From this point of view, although the second position may be considered Marxist, the first (regardless of whether it is factually true or false) is neither peculiarly "Marxist" nor "anti-Marxist." Although it expresses a thesis obviously contradictory to the results of Marx's own research, it is based, legitimately or not, on a rule which, though Marx used it, is not unique to his work. In other cases it is possible to question certain of Marx's theses by applying methodological rules that he not only used but used in a particular and distinctive way. We may call an analysis of this kind "Marxist" in a legitimate sense of the term.

Thus we come to the formulation of the problem under discussion. Marx's work contains essential features that are not peculiar to him and his followers, and that do not suffice to distinguish a separate school of thought: a relentlessly rationalist orientation, a sense of radical criticism, a distaste for sentimentality in social research, a deterministic method. Social scientists who fail to observe these principles—as the majority of people who called themselves Marxists notoriously and demonstrably did, in breach of the elementary rules of methodological rationalism—are surely not Marxists. (Instead, they easily may, and did, discredit the very idea of Marxism by associating it inseparably with their own methods of thinking and with the activities of the Office. At the same time, they made those who apply Marx's scientific contributions to their work ashamed of being called Marxist.) On the other hand, those who respect these principles do not thereby become Marxists, for these principles are not uniquely characteristic of Marx's work.

Yet there are many aspects of his work which constitute an original contribution to the development of the social sciences. They are, above all, certain methodological rules that enable man to know and master social material. The principle of determinism —and determinism becomes more intelligible if it is understood as a rule of thinking and not as a metaphysical theory—is certainly not specifically Marxist. It does not state simply that "In the same conditions the same phenomena occur," and still less that "all events are causally conditioned," because in such a formulation determinism becomes an empty generalization, unverifiable and fruitless in scientific research. Broadly speaking, this principle requires that we try to analyze every phenomenon as thoroughly as possible—given the tools and tasks at hand—by situating it within the framework of every kind of relationship with other phenomena. On the other hand, what is distinctively Marxist is a certain more specific conception of determinism, as expressed by the fundamental idea of historical materialism: the requirement that in a genetic analysis of political institutions and various forms of social consciousness we should look for the relationships that link them with social divisions arising from the system of ownership, or more generally, from the system of production; and for these we should seek the relationships connecting them with technical progress.

To be scientifically useful, such a principle must be formulated in general terms. It is, for instance, extremely harmful to interpret this principle as holding that fundamental class structure (in Marx's sense) determines *unequivocally* all other divisions in the social institutions and intellectual life of society throughout the entire history of mankind.

As we have said, what is typical of Marx is the tendency to emphasize the primary divisions in society that most influence the development of history. Also typical is his awareness of the limitations and distortions imposed on the social sciences by the pressures of societal conditions that shape the minds of researchers, as well as his fight to destroy ideological myths in science, a fight we never expected to have to resume most forcefully against a doctrine disguised under his name. Typical, too, is a certain type of historicism which not only rejects attempts to evaluate historical phenomena from the viewpoint of a moralistic keeper of eternal values, but which is based on the general principle of the historical relativity of the subjects under study, and also on the conviction that human nature is the product of man's social history and that our entire conception of the world is "socially subjective." This means it is a product of collective activity, which creatively organizes reality to adapt it to man's biological and social orientation in the world, and only thus formed does it remain in our minds. In this sense, then, the whole extrahuman world is created by man.

Another typical trait is Marx's practical orientation in the social sciences. He selected problems to be dealt with according to whether they served the cause of an egalitarian society, the cause of abolishing class divisions and of emancipating the exploited and oppressed. Equally typical is his conviction that, on the strength of historical law, the capitalist economy and the political rule of the bourgeoisie will inevitably change into a socialist system, and that this transformation will take place as a result of the proletariat's rise to power. In time, the proletariat will abolish itself as a class, which will mean the abolition of classes as such and of the state as an instrument of class rule.

And so we have an enumeration—only as illustrations, of course —of the principles and conclusions that are connected specifically with the name of Marx in the history of science. We are speaking here exclusively about matters dealing with the methodology of the social sciences, for there is no typical Marxist methodology which has affected the development of the natural sciences (with the exception of Marxist methodology in the official meaning of the term, which successfully helped deter progress).

It is not difficult to see that many of these rules have been permanently assimilated into the social sciences as practiced by groups totally independent of official Marxism, and therefore considered by the Office as non-Marxist, anti-Marxist, bourgeois, and so on. Many of Marx's ideas entered into the bloodstream of scientific life and thus ceased to distinguish Marx—and those who regarded themselves as orthodox believers in his doctrine—from others. From this point of view, then, dividing scientists into Marxists and non-Marxists became entirely meaningless. Still, there are other significant elements of Marx's method which have not become so widely accepted and at least appear to provide the basis for making such a distinction. But the question is not that simple, and for several reasons.

First of all, the word "Marxism," as it is commonly used and most deeply rooted in today's social consciousness, is linked with an intellectual activity that is notorious in philosophy and sociology. I mean it is used in the first of the two meanings discussed above—the institutional sense associated with the activity of the Office. It is clear that no lay sociologist or philosopher with scientific aspirations has the slightest wish to have anything in common with Marxism thus conceived because he does not like to be accused of religiosity. Therefore, even if his scientific work is most profoundly inspired by Marx, he is either very reluctant to describe his outlook as Marxist or else he must, in each instance, define precisely his use of the term.

That is why in order to revitalize the distinction between Marxists and non-Marxists the first condition would be to disseminate a concept of Marxism different from the current one. The possibility of such a revision, however, depends on certain social facts. This is so because the meaning of words is a social fact and cannot be established arbitrarily by simply declaring that we wish to practice "true" Marxism, while up till now the majority of Marxists were really pseudo-Marxists, Marxists in quotation marks. (This explains why, in speaking of intellectual Stalinism, I am not trying to present it as a sort of pseudo-Marxism in contradistinction to some kind of genuine Marxism. For Stalinism created a socially vital concept of Marxism that was an institutional and not an intellectual phenomenon, and this concept did function successfully in reality. There was only one element of mystification in it: the name of Karl Marx, from which the term was originally derived. But as time passes, etymological associations die out or at least grow fainter in the minds of people using a given term.)

Second, and even more important, outside and independently of the existence and functioning of institutional Marxism, there emerged in the social sciences a variety of conceptual categories, methodological rules, and new—now highly developed—branches of study. Therefore, in the intellectual sense of Marxism, there are whole areas of research where the division between Marxists and non-Marxists never assumed any significance. Obviously we should not infer from this that Marx's method, even today, would be irrelevant and unable to provide a vigorous and dynamic inspiration for research in these fields. If, for example, sociological investigations of public opinion developed almost entirely outside the sphere of influence of the Marxist tradition, still it is very likely that new perspectives for study in this realm could be opened if its fundamental stock of categories were enriched by the introduction of Marx's concept of class. Since logical semantics has made use of tools that ignore the social aspect of meaning, here Marx's method of analysis could probably contribute in many ways to its progress. In many fields of research, particularly in political and economic history as well as in the history of various areas of culture, Marx's theoretical achievements have played a significantly creative role, and this in spite of institutional Marxism. Hence it would obviously be absurd, merely because of the long existence of institutional Marxism, to advocate a return to Ranke's type of historiography, Kallenbach's history of literature, and Zeller's history of philosophy.

Third and finally, we must note that if the decision whether a given doctrine, theory, or historical interpretation is Marxist or non-Marxist is to make any sense at all, that decision can be based only on a consideration of the very general methodological assumptions used to construct that doctrine or theory. Of course, the borderline between a "fact" and an "interpretation" is flexible and defies precise definition in the social sciences, just as in the natural ones. Nonetheless, there does exist a great mass of knowledge whose "factual" character is beyond any doubt, and to call it "Marxist" is nonsense.

On the other hand, the history of science teaches us that problems of interpretation are never settled with any finality. The best proof of this is provided by an obvious fact that casts doubt on the primitive belief that it is possible to achieve complete objectivity in the social sciences—the fact that nearly every human generation rewrites the history of the world. What is noteworthy is that this is very often done successfully. And this means that the same, or nearly the same, stock of factual knowledge lends itself to a great number of well-founded and rationally justified— though radically different—interpretations. Is it worthwhile to take the trouble to determine whether they are Marxist or not, and if so, in which cases?

From the point of view of institutional Marxism, the matter is clear: In 1945 the only Marxist evaluation of Hegel was that he was a German chauvinist, an apologist for war, an enemy of the Slavic peoples, and a precursor of fascism; in 1954 Hegel had become an eminent dialectician, an idealist who played an important role in shaping Marx's philosophy. From the standpoint of an intellectual conception of Marxism, the problem looks somewhat different. There does not exist, and never will, one "truly Marxist" interpretation of Stoic philosophy, or a particular interpretation of Mickiewicz's poetry that would be "the only one compatible with Marxism." One can speak of interpreting Stoic philosophy with the help of general Marxist rules of historical methodology, but the same method may yield widely differing results. For the hope that the methodology of the social sciences may come to resemble a logarithmic table or a computer that will always enable us to proceed from a given set of facts to the same unequivocal answers is a chimera. Moreover, it is far from certain that the most rigorous application of this methodology would necessarily lead to conclusions in agreement with some particular remarks of Friedrich Engels about Stoicism—nor can it exhaust the possibilities of scientific study of the subject.

That is why disputes in which scholars try to snatch from each other the exclusive privilege of using "genuine Marxism" and to monopolize the honorable title of "consistent Marxist" are sterile verbalism. One can argue whether a given theory fulfills more or less well the requirements of scientific thinking, which include the essential rules of the method worked out by Marx. These rules, however, must be of a very general nature, and they do not contain any specific instructions on how to evaluate one or another historical phenomenon. Moreover, they always allow for many possible interpretations: the rule of historical materialism itself does not determine the type, intensity, or degree of uniformity of the influence exerted by the sum total of material conditions of life on the social thinking of people in all the epochs of history. And, *a forteriori*, historical materialism does not deter-

184 / *Toward a Marxist Humanism*

mine whether, for example, Pascal's philosophy is to be taken as an expression of the decadent tendencies of declining feudalism, or a representation of bourgeois thought, or something else again. In sociological investigations, and even more so in philosophical ones, there is hardly a single perfectly unambiguous term. Vacillations in meaning are inherited by even the most fundamental theses of a doctrine; none can be regarded as precise. If terms such as "matter," "social consciousness," "cognition," "superstructure," "causal determination," "relations of production," and so on are not clear, it follows that no methodological rules and no assertions of the theory in which they are involved have a precisely defined meaning.

Therefore, what we call Marxism, as understood in its intellectual function and as a method of thinking, can vary greatly in content within the limits of a very general framework. We know that it would be difficult to develop a Marxist angelology, and that we certainly could not present Bossuet's philosophy of history as Marxist. To know this, however, is not very useful, since our primary purpose in using the word "Marxist" is not to distinguish scientific thinking from the notorious irrationalism of theologians. The fact is that within the boundaries of science, where various styles of thinking and various types of methodology can very well coexist and compete, the borderline between Marxism and non-Marxism is extremely fluid.

It is obvious that it cannot be otherwise in view of at least two circumstances mentioned earlier—the insufficiency for contemporary scholarship of the rules Marx formulated, as well as their ambiguity; and also the fluidity of the limits of their validity. Thus to speak of a "compact and uniform Marxist camp," in contradistinction to the rest of the world, defining by its very existence a basic line of division in science, or to proclaim shibboleths about the "purity of Marxist doctrine"—all this makes no sense in the intellectual conception of Marxism. It may have a certain utility, but only when Marxism is considered as a political or religious phenomenon rather than as a science. In circumstances where we must venture to separate knowledge from faith, as the Averroists did against orthodoxy in the thirteenth century, and where political tactics become less and less able to exert their destructive pressure on the content of scientific knowledge, the Marxist "camp" in science will increasingly assume an ethereal shape instead of remaining the monolithic mass it once was. Of course, the tradition of the old, rigid division into Marxists and non-Marxists is not defunct, and will certainly influence scientific life for a long time to come, even where institutional Marxism is dead and discredited in the social consciousness. It is equally certain, though, that the pressure of this tradition will continue to decrease in direct proportion to the gradual elimination of institutional Marxism from the realm of science.

This does not in the least imply that in the humanistic sciences—those inevitably most influenced by social conditions —all divisions caused by differing world views have ceased to exist. But the most significant division is not that between orthodox Marxists guarding the purity of the doctrine against any admixture of heathen blood on the one hand, and everyone else on the other. It is—to use political language for a moment—the division between the Right and the Left in the humanities. This cleavage is most often characterized less by a concrete methodology than by an intellectual attitude. By the intellectual Left in the humanities we mean intellectual activity distinguished by: radical rationalism in thinking; steadfast resistance to any invasion of myth into science; an entirely secular view of the world; criticism pushed to its utmost limits; distrust of all closed doctrines and systems; striving for open-mindedness, that is, readiness to revise accepted theses, theories, and methods; esteem for scientific innovation; tolerance toward differing scientific standpoints, together with a simultaneous preparedness for war—even one of aggression—against every manifestation of irrationalism; and above all, a belief in the cognitive values of science and in the possibility of social progress.

Like all such delimitations, this one is less exact than, say, a national boundary. Still, it seems to me incomparably more significant than the division that the traditional Marxist camp has traditionally accepted. Wherever these attitudes prevail, they are enough to guarantee that all Marx's scientific contributions—

whose importance for the humanities cannot be overrated—will be preserved and perpetuated in scientific thought. These attitudes also make it possible to decide what is obsolete in Marx's doctrine and what is rash generalization, disproved by subsequent history. For today it is clear that several of Marx's ideas have not survived the merciless test of time. His predictions as to the future course of history, especially, were as fallible as most predictions are. Such ideas retain only the significance of utopias, that of moral stimulus rather than scientific theory.

Moreover, we can assume that with the gradual refinement of research techniques in the humanities, the concept of Marxism as a separate school of thought will in time become blurred and ultimately disappear altogether, just as there is no "Newtonism" in physics, no "Linnaeism" in botany, no "Harveyism" in physiology, and no "Gaussism" in mathematics. What is permanent in Marx's work will be assimilated in the natural course of scientific development. In the process some of his theses will surely be restricted in scope, others will be more precisely formulated, still others discarded. But the greatest triumph of an eminent scholar comes when his achievements cease to define a separate school of thought, when they merge into the very tissue of scientific life and become an elemental part of it, losing their disparate existence. This process is obviously different and much slower in the humanities, but even there it is an essential part of progress.

It is otherwise in the field of philosophy, taken as a discursive expression of a view of the world. There, names of great creative thinkers live through the centuries in the names of trends and schools of thought—yet they change character. When we use the term "Platonism" to describe a particular contemporary tendency in philosophy, we are not referring to orthodox believers in the whole Platonic doctrine, because there are none. "Platonism" in the current philosophical context applies to a more or less distant affinity with the particular ideas that have survived as the most distinctive and characteristic features of Plato's thought: belief in the primacy of the species over the individual; belief in the double existence of things—one sensate and forever changing, the other inaccessible to direct observation, immutable.

In the history of world views one can scarcely imagine a total disappearance of doctrinal variety and a rigid monopoly by one system. That is why terms derived from the names of those who introduced into philosophy original and revealing perspectives or formulated widely accepted points of view will surely survive. "Marxism" in this sense does not denote a doctrine that must be accepted or rejected as a whole. It does not mean a universal system, but a vital philosophical inspiration affecting our whole outlook on the world, a constant stimulus to the social intelligence and social memory of mankind. It owes its permanent validity to the new and invaluable points of view it opened before our eyes, enabling us to look at human affairs through the prism of universal history; to see, on the one hand, how man in society is formed by the struggle against nature and, on the other hand, the simultaneous process by which man's work humanizes nature; to consider thinking as a product of practical activity; to unmask myths of consciousness as resulting from ever recurring alienations in social existence and to trace them back to their real sources. These perspectives enable us, furthermore, to analyze social life in its incessant conflicts and struggles which, through countless multitudes of individual goals and desires, individual suffering and disappointments, individual defeats and victories, together compose a picture of uniform evolution that—we have every right to believe—signifies, on the grand scale of history, not retrogression but progress.

Determinism and Responsibility

In broaching this supremely classic subject I do not intend either to defend or to question any form whatsoever of a deterministic view of the world. I merely wish to bring home the common logical situation of two concepts that are chronically presented as *logically contradictory*: determinism and moral responsibility.

Nor will we consider another topic, whose discussion often replaces an analysis of the real difficulty that concerns us: the efficacy and validity of punishment, given the postulate of determinism. For we regard as prejudged in the affirmative the matter of whether, assuming the premise of determinism—no matter how rigorously conceived—punishment can be effective, if one admits that it is either a form of social self-defense designed to immobilize elements that a particular society considers dangerous, or a means of preventing through fear deeds like those punished, or else an educational tool. Yet it is an obvious truth—and indeed, one repeated too often over the centuries—that if one believes punishment thus defined can be effective, then one posits by that very fact some kind of determinism of human behavior, and absolute determinism is not excluded. The question whether one can believe in both determinism and the efficacy of punishment without conflict is therefore banal; and we do not mean to substitute it for the question of possible noncontradictory acceptance of both determinism and moral responsibility—which is not at all banal and which has no obvious answer.

This question also ceases to be banal to the degree that penal action is taken not in one of the three interpretations cited above but as an *act of revenge* that demands *moral validity*. The decision whether anyone is morally authorized to wreak vengeance, assuming the unequivocal determinism of human behavior, depends on the settlement of a broader issue: the logical consistency or inconsistency between the premise of unequivocal determinism and the affirmation that human behavior can with authority be

188

morally evaluated by others. This dependence is such that a positive answer to the second question is a necessary condition, though not the only one, for a positive reply to the first. In other words, whoever concedes that people can be morally empowered to commit acts of vengeance cannot, without contradiction, refrain from admitting as well that they are authorized to judge morally the behavior of others; whoever negates the second also negates the first; whoever accepts the first also accepts the second. However, the reverse does not hold, that is, that whoever denies the former also denies the latter; or that whoever affirms the latter also affirms the former. In any case, we shall disregard the question of the moral authority of acts of vengeance given the assumption of determinism, contenting ourselves with a consideration of the more general subject of the validity, in these circumstances, of the admission that moral responsibility exists.

But before we try to phrase this question in a form appropriate to our intended sphere of discussion, let us formulate the following premises as a preliminary to our analysis without a complete explication of the concepts involved, for we believe that they are either adequately established in the literature on the subject or else sufficiently clear on the basis of intuition.

In the first premise, we repeat the now classic truth that normative statements are not equivalent to statements of judgment and are not implied by them alone, that is, without the additional premise of other normative statements.[1] (The difficulties that sometimes arise in differentiating between these two kinds of statement are not pertinent here, for we will be dealing with statements that should be clearly one kind or the other.)

In the second premise we wish to determine if and in what sense a contrary situation can arise—one in which certain normative pronouncements can imply adjudicative statements. To this end, we introduce the concept of the sense or nonsense of a norm,

---

1. *The Bases of a Science of Morality*, by Maria Ossowska (Warsaw, 1947), comprises, especially in Chapters IV and V, a detailed and precise survey of all the arguments in favor of this view, as well as against it. Agreeing with the conclusions of the author, we shall not elaborate further on this problem.

in a somewhat unusual definition. The statement that a norm is nonsense may be understood in any one of three ways. First, it may be a matter of the contradiction of the sense ascribed to all adjudicative declarations as such: in this meaning, one can recognize as nonsense all normative expressions. Second, we may use the term nonsense in exactly the same way as when we speak of all statements, that is, as a mixture of semantic categories, or the utilization of expressions unauthorized in the lexicon of a given language.

Third—and this is the meaning we have in mind—nonsense may be conceived as a situation in which a given norm poses a demand that cannot possibly be either fulfilled or violated in view of the actual contingencies of reality to which it applies. One can say that in such an event the norm implies certain false premises; more precisely, here it is not a matter of a logical derivation of adjudicative statements from normative ones, but of the derivation of certain affirmations about reality from the affirmation that judges that a particular norm makes sense. The latent assumption behind normative statements is the judgment that reality allows for the possibility both of carrying out the action recommended by a given norm, and of not carrying it out. A norm makes sense when it can be either realized or broken within the context of the contingencies and laws that operate in the world of the people it is supposed to rule. Thus a Biblical commandment forbidding the eating of griffins would be a nonsense norm because it could not be broken. Equally nonsensical would be the commandment to eat griffins in certain situations, because it could not be obeyed. Consequently we grant that a sensible norm, or rather, simply a norm, makes a certain assumption about reality: that reality is so constructed that it permits people moving within it to act either in accordance or not in accordance with the norm's positive or negative demand. A nonsense norm, or a pseudonorm, requires us to perform or to desist from performing acts of which, given the properties of the world in which these acts or this desistance are to take place, one alternative is impossible: either behavior in accordance with the norm, or else behavior contrary to it.

Third assumption: The negation of a norm is a norm.[2]

In our fourth assumption we wish, without further elaborations of the concept of responsibility, to turn our attention to the difference between this concept and that of perpetration. It is one thing to "be responsible" and quite another to "be the perpetrator." Perpetration is a physical category, responsibility a moral one. (We are not using "responsibility" in the familiar sense in which *with respect to facts that have already occurred* one terms "responsible" the person whose acts or the consequences thereof are *evaluated negatively*; that is, not in the sense that allows the statement that someone is responsible for another's death but agrees only reluctantly to the declaration that someone is responsible for saving another's life or for the writing of a good scholarly work. We prefer the convention that admits the concept of responsibility for the consequences of acts regardless of the nature of the evaluation placed on those consequences.) The person responsible for a given event is not necessarily its physical perpetrator, but the person who, in his social situation, had the *duty* to undertake action which would cause or prevent a given result and who did or did not do so. A doctor who has killed a patient by injecting an incorrectly manufactured medication is in the physical sense the perpetrator of the death. He is not, however, responsible for it since his duty was to carry out the right treatment, not to verify the chemical composition of the medicine. Responsibility

---

2. This assumption may give rise to a doubt stemming from the conviction that normative statements are negated in two ways. A certain *command* expressed as "ought . . ." can be negated by an *interdiction* expressed as "may not. . . ." It can also be negated by the ascertainment that the situation to which a given norm applies is neutral as regards obligation, that is, that this specific action "may" or "may not" be done in terms of the accepted system of values. If the normative character of the first negation ("may not . . .") arouses no doubts, then they may be aroused by the normative character of the second ("may . . . ," "has the right . . . ," "is permissible . . ."). In our opinion, which we will not justify further here, the statement that certain actions in certain conditions may be either performed or not performed—that they are indifferent from the point of view of the accepted system of values—also has a normative nature and possesses characteristics required of normative statements, among others that it cannot be justified otherwise than by recourse to that very system of accepted values.

is therefore contingent upon duty—that is, upon the complex of norms, fixed by morality or accepted on the basis of custom, that govern specific situations in which people find themselves.[3] Thus conflicts in ascertaining moral responsibility do not stem from the difficulty of establishing the physical cause of certain consequences, but from the fact that there do not and cannot exist in any society complexes of norms and rules about obligations that describe the respective duty situations in a way that would permit us to decide unequivocally in each concrete case whether such a situation had indeed arisen.

After these introductory premises, let us try to consider where the difficulty lies in the question that interests us, and exactly what the popular objections are that point out the supposed contradiction between the admission that moral responsibility exists and the avowal that reality has a deterministic character.

As to the true sense of the concept of determinism, we shall bypass this area and confine ourselves to the familiar meaning, noting, however, that if we differentiate three main groups among all the various interpretations of this concept—methodological, phenomenalistic, and metaphysical—those popular objections do not in any case apply to the first. That is, they have nothing to do with the understanding of determinism solely as a rule of intellectual procedure that bids us relate every object of study to the greatest possible number of other objects, thus establishing a sequence of dependencies about whose nature we assert nothing. Obviously, determinism so conceived is logically independent of the question of moral responsibility; for we see it not as a thesis about reality, but merely as a rule of thought and research. The

---

3. In this connection I believe Tadeusz Kotarbinski's definition of perpetration in *A Treatise on Good Work* (Lodz, 1955), Chapter II, can be defended against the objection that according to his definition one is not necessarily responsible for the deeds one perpetrates: this combination actually does not occur, but in my opinion that is no reason for arguing against the definition of the concept of perpetration which holds that "the perpetrator of a given occurrence is he whose gratuitous impulse is the cause of that occurrence" (p. 30), and that the cause, in turn, is the actual component of the condition that is sufficient for a given event to occur at a given moment and in terms of some innate regularity in the order of events (p. 27).

authorization for this regulation—that is, for the assumption that justifies the efficacy of applying it—can be determinism either in the phenomenalist sense (formulated, for example, as "In the same conditions the same phenomena occur") or in the metaphysical version, variously phrased but always affirming the existence of a universal causal connection on the strength of which a gratuitous event is unequivocally designated causative by the sum total of conditions in which it takes place. Realizing that each of the words used in such formulations poses unlimited question marks, and also that the search for material proof encounters insurmountable difficulties, we do not propose to engage in discussion of these matters. We are satisfied with the awareness that in both the phenomenalist and the metaphysical versions, the principle of determinism is involved in that apparent or real conflict whose true substance we wish to ascertain.

Advocates of the view that this conflict is real and insuperable reason somewhat this way: Determinism means that whatever happens *cannot* not happen; it follows that whatever any individual man has done, he *could not have done* otherwise. This being so, we are not authorized morally to condemn or approve his deeds, which are admittedly inevitable, and thus to burden him with moral responsibility for his behavior.

Let us try to weigh the meaning of this argument more precisely.

The first stage of this line of reasoning ("whatever happens cannot not happen") can be stated thus: The nonoccurrence of any given event in the conditions in which it actually did occur would be contradictory to the regulations which, regardless of our knowledge, govern the reality "in and of itself" in which that event happens. This is an approximate definition, but sufficient for the needs of this discussion.

The next step requires greater care. What do we actually mean when we say "People are morally responsible for their deeds"? Surely not the trite observation that they are *regarded* by others as responsible, that people in general judge others' behavior morally. In this sense such a statement, whose truth needs no substantiation, can have nothing in common with the principle of determinism except the reflection that since determinism of human actions is universal, then actions consisting of the moral evaluation of others or of oneself, or ascribing responsibility to them or to oneself, and therefore assigning *obligation*, are just as determined as all the rest.

Defenders of the thesis that there is a conflict between determinism and responsibility have something completely different in mind. They say that the determinist as such is *unauthorized* to ascribe moral responsibility to people. Now then, to hold that people are morally responsible means that *on the whole something is the object of obligation*, that is, that certain actions *ought* to be performed in certain circumstances, and that others *ought not*. In turn, the statement that something is the object of obligation has a normative nature, for normative statements are those which we can acknowledge only after we have affirmed that something is the object of obligation, or else those from which an obligation is derived in the sense in which a result relationship arises between normative observations. But since there is no doubt that in order to recognize an object of obligation one must believe that there is an object of obligation, this statement has a normative character. We might call it a pre-norm, in the sense that it is actually the affirmation of the very validity of recognizing norms.

This being so, then in accordance with our previously formulated third assumption, the negation of this statement is also normative. In other words, the statement "It is not true that something is the object of obligation" is a norm.

In this fashion we come to the conclusion that the position we are considering depends on a result relationship between the principle of determinism—in either of the two versions we have mentioned, which we cannot doubt fill a descriptive function—and the normative statement denying that anything can be the object of obligation; the normative statement is implied by the descriptive one. Now on the basis of our first assumption, a result relationship of this type cannot occur, and the position in question looks untenable because it contradicts the logical normative statements that modern science has propagated and society has accepted.

Moreover, partisans of the opposite view fall into a typical antinomy, analogous to that of the liar. This antinomy springs from a situation logically independent of the premises on which one formulates the thesis "It is not true that something is the object of obligation"—that is, independent of the fact that they believe this negation results from the principle of universal causality. But if a general negation of the validity of norms is itself a norm, then whoever proclaims this negation performs an act whose essence is the prohibition of just such acts. In reality, to say "People are not morally responsible" is to say that no obligation is morally valid, that *no one has the right* to judge anything morally, either to condemn or to approve. But in saying this we merely put a ban on uttering bans; we judge negatively the fact of a negative or positive judgment. We then fall into a practical contradiction like that of a man writing a book to demonstrate that one should not write books, or someone who kills men because they oppose the idea that one should not kill, and the like. For this reason it does not seem possible without contradiction to demand, on any basis, that one refrain from using normative statements.

Unfortunately, we cannot close our discussion at this point without adding: *Quod erat demonstrandum*. For there is also a way to the conflict we are considering that renders it immune to removal by the means we have just cited.

Let us look more closely at the actual practical functioning of the thesis that sees a logical link between the principle of determinism and the principle of responsibility. Why is our sense of what is right not disturbed by the fact that jurisprudence, in almost all modern criminal codes, uses such categories as "limited responsibility" and "absence of responsibility" for certain acts that appear to a sound mind to be "more determined," or "less the fault of the perpetrator"? If punishment can be abolished or reduced for the psychologically ill, the mentally deficient, or even people in what we call a state of temporary insanity, doesn't this tacitly admit the link whose nonexistence we strove to demonstrate? Would these distinctions lose their significance if we accepted the principle of causality in a version in which the actions of each man in each situation would presumably be determined to the same degree?

Noting beforehand that this answer seems inadequate, one could say in reply that the difference between people of so-called limited responsibility and those of what is termed full responsibility is not moral, but purely technical. Criminal law does not belong to the domain of morality and is not dependent upon it. Its tasks are practical, to devise the most efficient methods of preventing or rendering harmless acts which are socially dangerous. Perhaps that is why in postulating the same degree of determinism for all human deeds, we postulate at the same time that given different determinations it is most efficient socially to vary repressive reactions against perpetrators. If a murder resulting from delusions of persecution can provoke the reaction of confining the perpetrator in an asylum, whereas a premeditated murder committed by a normal person is punished by long years of imprisonment, then the difference in the handling of the two cases need not stem at all from a belief that the normal person's behavior was more a matter of "free choice" or less determined than that of the madman. In this instance, a prison and a psychiatric hospital are the same, from the point of view of the moral assumptions indispensable to the building of prisons or hospitals; in both cases we need no assumptions other than the general belief that, to the greatest extent possible, one should reduce the physical liberty of individuals dangerous to the collectivity. Prisons and hospitals are merely two types of techniques performing their assignment in two different types of human situations. One simply assumes that certain means work better with sick persons and others with normal ones, if the aim is the same—to free society from the threat posed when such individuals are under no physical restraint. The situation of a man locked in a hospital and that of a man punished by prison do not differ from a moral point of view, but only technically. Punishment does not require moral sanction; a practical sanction suffices.

We repeat that this argument does not appear adequate to us. Such an interpretation is obviously possible, yet what we were asking was if and why we are not disturbed by the differentiation of legal reactions to deeds of people who have been determined in different ways. The actual legal interpretation of this differentiation is different, for what it uses is precisely the concept of responsibility, and not of perpetration, as its basis. If in both cases the perpetration is unquestionable, the responsibility is still assumed to be different, as in the fourth of our preliminary assumptions. In fact, both in law and in popular opinion we admit that we are dealing with differentiated responsibility, that is, with differentiated *obligation,* ascribed to the perpetrators on the grounds of the kind of determination to which their behavior is subject. If this is so, we tacitly assume a connection between a deterministic interpretation of behavior and the possibility of judging it morally; in other words, we assume that a condition for such judgment is that one treats human actions as determined by a "free" choice and as therefore, at some stage in their realization or preparation, spontaneous.

To this, in turn, one may reply that if popular opinion, so deeply rooted in society's consciousness, actually treats the matter thus, it is by no means proof that such treatment is right; for we all, in spite of ourselves, are victims of the same mystification that is inculcated by traditional images of the conditions surrounding human actions.

We digress at this point not in order to make our decision on the main question easier, but only to show that the practical significance of this subject may be different from what one sometimes thinks. It is in fact, as we have said, incontrovertible that all punishment can be executed quite independently of how the importance of the principle of universal causality is evaluated. And yet the question of whether there is any real difference between social upbringing and the training of dogs is not without a certain practical relevance. It is easy to understand that the very fact of the existence and operation in the social consciousness of such phenomena as the sense of obligation and the affirmation of certain values—no matter to what extent we may wish to legalize them—is an essential, indispensable weapon of self-defense for every kind of social bond against destructive agents. It is hard to imagine a society in which human deeds did not encounter reactions invoking concepts of "obligation" and "responsibility," yet in which, at the same time, they did meet with reactions sufficiently efficacious to counteract destructive factors. In other words, elemental moral opinions have so far been irreplaceable as a natural tool of society's attempt to preserve itself, its conatus ad suum esse conservandum. In saying that the concept of responsibility cannot validly be used we do not, it is true, question the need to employ the means by which various collectivities react to prevent destruction of the devices that keep them alive; but we do take away from these means, at least in theory, one of the most effective factors, the moral consciousness of the collectivity as it reacts to the behavior of its components.

To return now to our main subject, we have said that the conflict between determinism and the recognition of responsibility can be interpreted so as to prevent a situation in which normative statements must be derived from judgments that are not norms. In fact, we can accept the idea that the situation described in our second assumption arises here—one in which a normative negation of responsibility does not result from the principle of determinism, whereas the negation of determinism proceeds from a normative affirmation of responsibility. In this sense, if it could be upheld, the affirmation of responsibility, which means a judgmental statement that "Something is the object of obligation," would become nonsense if the principle of determinism were true; whereas the negation of this principle, and thus a false judgment, would then be implied by this normative statement. If such a logical connection arises, whoever recognizes the principle of determinism is not by that token forced to express a general negative norm; but he must, on the other hand, recognize a general positive or negative norm to be nonsense. Our task, therefore, is to ascertain whether such a connection does not in fact occur.

In accordance with our second assumption, a norm is nonsense when the obligation postulated by it cannot be both carried out and not carried out in terms of the reality in which people perform the actions this norm regulates. In the case that interests us, it is a matter of the confrontation of the most generalized normative statement, "Something is the object of obligation," with the principle which holds that, for example, "In the same conditions the same phenomena occur."

The norm that concerns us is actually an expression with variables related to a smaller quantifier: it means that conditions C′ and C″ exist, as well as actions A′ and A″, so that in conditions C′ there is the obligation to perform action A′, and in conditions C″ there is the obligation to prevent action A″. In agreement with the premise above, this statement becomes nonsense if two requirements are met: The first depends on the fact that the statement implies that there exist in general actions A which in conditions C can be both performed and not performed; we consider this requirement fulfilled. The second requirement holds that from the principle of determinism, in the formulation we have cited, there results the fact that this last statement is false—that there are no human actions A which in conditions C can be both performed and not performed. The objections in question are then valid; that is, determinism entails the negation of responsibility if it is true that the statement "In the same conditions the same phenomena occur" gives rise to the statement "There are no human actions which in the same conditions can be both performed and not performed."

As one can easily see, the whole difficulty of the problem hinges on that little word "can," which concentrates in itself most of the knotty questions connected with the philosophical interpretation of determinism. Unwilling to sink into bottomless depths, we will content ourselves with the following observation:

To say that action A cannot not occur in conditions C means that its nonoccurrence in these conditions would require that the validity operative in the reality in which these conditions exist would not hold. Once again we formulate the situation in terms that in turn demand interpretation. Without even attempting it, we are nevertheless able to establish that if it is true that in the same conditions the same phenomena occur, then it is true that if in conditions C action A occurs, the supposition that there arises an action A′ which differs from A entails the supposition that this action occurs in conditions C′ which differ from C.

In other words, if there occur such conditions C that there arises action A as well as a different action A′, then it follows that conditions C are simultaneously the different conditions C′. (Needless to say, one of the components in the conditions as a whole is obviously the fact that the individual performing the action is identical in every respect.)

It would thus seem that the arguments in favor of the existence of a conflict between the principle of determinism and that of responsibility are correct, since the opposite assumption leads to a contradiction. But basically, the victory of the partisans of this line of reasoning is entirely superficial. Nevertheless, to disclose this superficiality requires recourse to the extra-formal side of the problem.

Let us reflect on what we had in mind and what we were concerned with earlier when we introduced the concept of a nonsense norm, a pseudonorm in this meaning. Since we introduced this concept on the strength of an arbitrary definition, we must justify it in terms of its usefulness in discussion of the methodology of normative disciplines. Our aim in formulating it was to present in the tersest possible form the popular objections which attribute "abolition of responsibility" to the deterministic position. Actually, we were trying to distinguish between norms that "can" have a practical pertinence and those that cannot because reality itself does not permit one of the alternatives, either the practical implementation of the norm, or else its nonimplementation. To put it otherwise, it was a matter of differentiating between norms whose promulgation, pronouncement, and propagation can be practically efficacious, because the properties of the world are such that these norms can be either implemented or not, and those norms whose promulgation, pronouncement, and propagation are practically inefficacious, because the properties of the world are such that, regardless of whether these norms are proclaimed or not, people are unequivocally determined by the situation in which they act to implement or not what the norm presents as the object of obligation.

Now let us ask if our reasoning has really led us to the conclusion that *all* norms are nonsense in this context—if, for example, the norm "One may not mistreat the weak" finds itself in the same situation as the norm "One may not eat griffins." The latter, whether it is proclaimed or not, cannot practically be broken, because griffins are mythical creatures. The former is, of course, sometimes observed, sometimes broken, which means that some conditions occur that facilitate its observance and others that are conducive to its being broken. But in the light of our previous reasoning, if every complex of concrete conditions unequivocally defines whether in those conditions this norm is or is not observed, then although it makes sense in the usual meaning of that word for all possible conditions, nevertheless it is nonsense in the context of every individual complex of concrete conditions. It might then, we repeat, seem that the promulgation of this norm, as of every other one, is *inefficacious*, since the human behavior to which it applies is carried out in each complex of concrete circumstances, regardless of whether it is promulgated or not. Only when this conclusion results from our prior line of thinking are we logically authorized to admit the correctness of arguments that maintain that "determinism abolishes responsibility."

It is easy to see that such a conclusion is not in the least indicated by our previous reasoning. If it is true that "In the same conditions the same phenomena occur," if in addition it is also true that in every complex of conditions in which any human action takes place, that action is not confronted with a number of possible courses but can take only one, then the very fact of promulgating, pronouncing, and propagating certain obligations or norms belongs to the complex of conditions in which human actions occur. If, therefore, one posits that these actions are determined, even in the most rigorous sense of the word, one does not by any means posit thereby that they cannot be determined or co-determined by the recognition in a given human collectivity of certain values expressed as obligations, prohibitions, commandments, norms. Since the most banal daily experience teaches us that the opposite is true—that the value judgments of human communities have a certain influence on the behavior of the individuals who comprise them—the matter appears unworthy of further consideration.

Thus it would seem that if the concept of the nonsense of norms that we introduced at the beginning is to retain its usefulness, it must be completed. We will call a nonsense norm a statement requiring the execution of or desistance from actions of which, given the properties of the world in which they are to occur, one of the alternatives is impossible: either behavior in accordance with the norm, or behavior contrary to that norm; and it is impossible *regardless of if and how this norm is promulgated, disseminated, or advocated.* We underline the phrase that completes the original definition, which in this form no longer implies that in accepting it we admit that a recognition of the deterministic view of the world cancels the possibility of belief in the efficacy of regulating human behavior by disseminating a faith in certain values.

We note two inferences from this line of reasoning: first, that determinism, even rigorously conceived, does not lead logically to the postulate of refraining from the use of moral judgments and norms; second, that it cannot be the premise for affirming that the use of moral judgments and norms is inefficacious as an attempt to regulate human actions in accordance with these norms and evaluations.[4]

---

4. We said at the beginning that we do not intend to substitute for the problem of the relationship between determinism and responsibility the problem of the efficacy of punitive actions, regarding the latter as prejudged in the affirmative. Meantime, it may seem that we have now brought the matter right back to the same query, replacing the question of moral *validity* with that of *efficacy.* To this possible objection we reply: First, our conclusion pertains not to the efficacy of punitive actions, but to the efficacy of promulgating and disseminating value judgments—which is not the same thing. Second, the first part of our deductions, summarized in the first of the two preceding inferences, aims to elucidate how the question under consideration can be asked in a way that makes sense. What results from it is that the principle of determinism in and of itself cannot logically lead us either to prohibit or to use moral evaluations and norms; and it has no logical connection with the question of their validity. After establishing this, we may ask if it leads to the conviction that promulgating value judgments

A disciple of the traditional line of argument that places determinism and responsibility in opposition could still object that, although determinism does allow us to admit that the promulgation of certain moral orders or bans can be efficacious, it does not allow us to admit that evaluations of behavior are "in and of themselves," regardless of our knowledge, morally good or bad; that determinism also permits us to proclaim the principle of responsibility, but does not permit us to recognize its "objectiveness," to acknowledge that in certain situations people are "objectively"—on the strength of the real properties of these situations, and not on the strength of the opinions of other people —obligated to perfom certain actions.

To which we reply: We accept the opinion that people are the sole creators of values, and we affirm this despite any espousal or negation of a deterministic view of the world. It is true that things "in themselves" are neither good nor bad, but are only so judged; this truth can be established without appeal to universal causality and remains a truth regardless of whether it is recognized as such. If, however, someone interprets the concept of "responsibility" and of "obligation" to mean that the responsible or obligated person can only be one who acts in a manner not determined by anything, then the argument that determinism does not permit us to accept responsibility without contradiction is pure tautology. But we see no reason that would compel us to understand the concept of responsibility or obligation in this sense. Nor do we see why morality should prove superfluous just because people behaving one way or another in situations recognized in their milieu as subject to moral qualification are determined or co-determined by awareness of values and by moral

---

is inefficacious in regulating human behavior, and to this question we reply negatively. In general, once one considers that moral convictions are part of the self-defensive behavior of the human race, any negation of their validity is—in accordance with the premise we have accepted—nonsense; that is, this negation, if interpreted normatively, falls exactly within the province of our definition of nonsense norms—those of which either the implementation or the nonimplementation (in this case, implementation) is impossible given the properties of the world to which they apply.

convictions, and do not act out of spontaneous and unlimited free choice. Why should an "authentically moral" act be one in which there is no determination—not even determination that results from an awareness of obligation that in turn results from the influence of values shaped by a given environment—whereas a deed motivated by moral convictions, and thereby determined, is not? No rational reply to this question presents itself. Hence there appears to be no reason which would constrain us to abide by the traditional argument that insists on a contradiction between a recognition of determinism and a recognition of moral values.

On the other hand, one can speculate on the real roots of the stubborn repetition of such objections in philosophical criticism. Their source is the interpretation of human behavior in the spirit of mechanistic determinism—for example, of the deterministic position in which *the facts of awareness are not taken into consideration as possible determinants of human behavior.* Speaking more loosely, mechanistic determinism posits that the self-knowledge of his own deeds on the part of a spontaneously acting human being boils down to an *observation* of his own behavior which has no influence on that behavior. A man's actions are wholly determined by the mechanical reactions of his physical structure to external mechanical stimuli; the circumstance that a man simultaneously *knows* what he is doing and *is conscious* of his own behavior creates in his mind the illusion of freedom of action, but has no real influence on his behavior.

In this interpretation, which has been anachronistic for centuries, it is easy to demonstrate that no influences on man's consciousness can alter his behavior; for the latter results from the inevitable universal automatisms of nature, which render any sort of normative ethics *inefficacious.* Regardless of his awareness of his own actions, and even of the values he has accepted or had inculcated by his upbringing, man is a mechanistic lump passively shunted about by the impact of neighboring lumps. The epiphenomenon of awareness merely helps the lump to perceive the movements of its body as an external observer. This conclusion is not required by the position that sees the facts of awareness as possible perpetrative factors in behavior, a position that obviously falls entirely within the realm of determinism, in spite of the enduring enigma of the links that bind the facts of awareness to all the processes observable by objective methods. This position, which postulates a differentiation of the facts of consciousness from others, lodges equally well inside the boundaries of the doctrine that says it is impossible to differentiate between the spirit and the flesh.

Let us permit ourselves, in connection with the question under discussion, two more rather loose comments. The formula "In the same conditions the same phenomena occur" is valuable when understood and applied as only an approximate construction, verifiable on the basis of patterns that in practice can be thought of as isolated although we know they are not so in fact. This construction is useful in cases when experiments carried out in conditions that pass as identical in practice yield perceptibly different results. Referring to this construction, we then surmise that identicalness of circumstances is less than we supposed, which induces us to seek the errors in our original premises. Without this postulate, explicitly or tacitly accepted, no methodical analysis of reality would be possible; thanks to it we know that if the phenomena we expect do not occur, the conditions of their occurrence are other than we supposed. The conditions we take into account in our investigations are always a pattern that we accept as isolated, and therefore fictitious; but which pattern we recognize as isolated depends on the nature of our practice and on the goals we wish to achieve, not on the real characteristics of this pattern. Choosing from the countless number of practical experiments and activities, we may, for example, regard the solar system as an isolated pattern and so omit from our prognostications regarding, and our analysis of, reality, influences coming from outside this pattern. But builders of interplanetary rockets, striving to protect them against cosmic rays, must include in their practical thinking the idea that in fact the solar system is not an isolated pattern. Thus our formula becomes less applicable as it becomes harder to distinguish among the phenomena under examination patterns we can recognize as practically isolated.

We cannot imagine a greater degree of such difficulty than the degree that prevails in the analysis of human behavior. Here it is truly hardest to establish which conditions, among the myriad possibilities, we may ignore and which we must consider. If we say that a phenomenon is determined, in the sense that its nonoccurrence in given conditions is incompatible with the laws of nature, then in practice it is a matter of using known rules to confront events that have occurred. In the great majority of human actions, no known laws of nature exclude the possibility that human behavior could have run a course other than it did in fact. In this situation a formula that informs us that if this course differed from what was expected, then "evidently" factors unknown to us intervened, is of little practical use. The role and dimensions of the perpetrative influence of the facts of consciousness on behavior are but slightly known. We posit, however, that an indispensable condition for treating people as responsible for their behavior is the consciousness of that behavior—that is, a situation in which it is possible for certain facts of consciousness, particularly moral convictions, to emerge as co-factors in the perpetration of the act. We recognize certain individuals as free from responsibility, not because we know that in a given situation they "could not have" behaved otherwise—whereas a normal person "could have" freely gone in a different direction—but because, according to the information at hand, the facts of moral consciousness are excluded as a co-factor.

In practice, then, the establishment of responsibility takes place without resort to universal determinism, and independently of it. As long as specific rules of causality in this realm of reality are inadequately known, the general principle of determinism is of little use here. It is better to treat this principle as a rule of scientific thinking that sets an unattainable goal: a limitless knowledge of all the dependencies in which the phenomenon under study is involved. But in scientific practice what is important is not so much the question "How should we take into consideration the general connection between things?" but "How can we ignore it most effectively?" That is, what patterns should we recognize as sufficiently isolated to be the subject of productive research? We know that the principle of general causality is not indispensable in designating such patterns, since we have already begun using them. Awareness of the principle is helpful to the degree that it induces us to seek the unperceived conditions of unexpected events. In this sense we may say that determinism is a condition of scientific thinking, but it is so as a rule of thought that contains certain values pertaining to philosophy and a view of the world—not as metaphysical knowledge of the nature of things. Determinism is, however, scientifically sterile and, of course, unprovable in a rigorous and literal sense.

Our last observation is historical. The conflict between determinism and morality has a hoary tradition. It was first voiced as a latent antinomy in the Stoic doctrine. On the one hand, "It is impossible"—in the words of Epictetus—"for things to run a different course than they actually pursue." It follows that the best an individual can do is adapt himself to inevitability, treating himself as an actor in a play someone else wrote and others take part in. "Do not ask that everything should happen as you wish, but wish that it should happen as it does. . . ." On the other hand, "In our power lie our attitudes, behavior, what we desire and what we avoid, in a word, every act that originates with us."

In this manner Stoicism turns to each man individually with the demand that he rid himself of an affective attitude toward the world and toward other people, on the principle that neither natural reality nor human reality can behave otherwise than they do. We must treat another man as a mechanism who is no more "guilty" when he wrongs us than a stone dislodged from a cliff by the wind. Simultaneously, the Stoic turns to each man individually with the demand that he treat himself as the only being with full command over his behavior, his thoughts, his deeds. Every human being must, following the summons of the Stoic, take upon himself the burden of all the freedom there is in the universe. Regarding himself as Epicurus' solitary atom in a Democritean cosmos, each must consider himself absolutely responsible and the world, just as absolutely, not responsible. Stoicism is knowledge of a freedom that serves only one man in the world, and that one is the man to whom the knowledge is directed, which means, in effect, every man.

This antinomy at the heart of Stoicism is ineradicable, and is the reason why Stoicism cannot be a doctrine of universal importance, but only a call to every individual consciousness. Each such appeal, taken literally, contradicts all the others, and moreover, no appeal is to be directed to other people. Each man has the right only to direct the appeal toward himself, since its essence is precisely such an affirmation of one's own freedom that when it is addressed to others it creates its own negation; it is the doing of something to which one denies value by this very act. The most authentic Stoicism is a monologue.

If Stoicism is more than that, it is not only as a result of inconsistency but also because Stoicism, regardless of its contradiction, advocates a position that ascribes value to individual life. It attempts to liberate daily life not from moral judgments as a whole, but from an affective attitude toward one's own fate, entangled as it is in independent environmental determinants. The Stoic-determinist need not stop judging the morality of people's behavior by applying abstract measures of right to it, but such evaluations are for him ordinary statements of fact; they are linked to no emotional excitation, they arouse in him no indignation, anger, sorrow, or despair. For it is true that deterministic convictions, if deeply and enduringly enough rooted in the consciousness of daily life, give birth to certain practical positions which are not to be scorned. There is no logical connection here, obviously, but a psychological one that is easily explained. It consists simply in the fact that an intense awareness of the inevitability of certain situations or events is actually often an effective means of countering the luxuriant overgrowth of affective attitudes toward them. We would certainly not consider useful a rule that urges a passive acceptance of the world in all its details on the premise that they are all allegedly equally inevitable. What can be useful is a rule that bids us test to what extent the material of human life is malleable, and that orders us to liberate ourselves spiritually as much as we can from everything that has in practice demonstrated its stubborn resistance to all change. Such reflections can be dangerous, for there are not many things that we can be sure are absolutely irrevocable, and to imagine a world of inevitability in dimensions larger than those warranted by experience is, in general, more harmful than to reduce those dimensions to the point where experience tells us to broaden them. Still, there exists at least one reality we can rightly consider inevitable: the reality of the past. And though our knowledge of the inevitablity of the past seems difficult to question in theory, in practice our attitudes toward life sometimes depend essentially on how much someone preoccupies himself with that banal subject. The Stoic doctrine can also be helpful from this point of view. Moreover, it becomes useful whenever we must draw practical conclusions from the recognition that our experience shows the world to be divided, above all, into things which are but need not be, plus all the others. One of the primordial experiences of mankind is a modal classification of reality. It is so widespread and so prosaic that it often goes unnoticed. The attempt to adapt oneself morally to this most common cognitive practice was a value perpetuated by Stoic thought throughout many centuries. Yet it is important that Stoicism teaches us that in the modal classification that each man makes for his own use, he must situate his own behavior in the world of possible things, not that of necessary things. This is not a knowledge solidly supported by theory, but the everyday empiricism of each individual human being, concerning him alone and therefore never susceptible of being transposed to a plane of general validity. It may be that in this interpretation the Stoic antinomy we discussed can be removed: that is to say, if we conceive its appeal not as a concealed thesis which one man expresses to himself—while at the same time denying it as a general principle—but as a summons to constant self-control in view of the division of the world we have postulated. If it then appears in the experience of each individual that his own conscious actions constitute for him a reality at the opposite extreme from the reality of past experience—that his actions do belong to the world of *possible* and evident things—still he has neither obligation nor cause to generalize his experience. Thus understood,

Stoicism could also be at least a guideline for deliberations intended to perpetuate both of the values—incorrectly treated as incompatible—we should like to defend: the belief in the absolute need for scientific, that is, causal, thinking, as well as the belief in the total responsibility of each human being for the part he plays in all the determinants at work in the humanized world, that is, quite simply, the world. For in human life the general knowledge that "everything that happens, happens inevitably" is not essential; nor is it essential—or possible—to kill the feeling of freedom of action which is peculiar to mankind. What is essential is a rational confrontation of human possibilities with the material of actions, the confrontation that gives rise, in the words of Lucretius, to the *fatis avulsa voluntas*, the will snatched from destiny. It need not be considered an unnatural break in the causal continuity of events, but an intervention of that causal perpetration which is also purposeful perpetration, and thus the action of nature which becomes conscious of itself.

In Praise of Inconsistency

I speak of consistency in one sense only, limited to the correspondence between behavior and thought, to the inner harmony between general principles and their application. Therefore I consider a consistent man to be simply one who, possessing a certain number of general, absolute concepts, strives earnestly in all he does, and in all his opinions about what should be done, to remain in the fullest possible accord with those concepts. A consistent man is one who considers killing evil and refuses to enter military service; one who is convinced of the superiority of monogamy over other forms of family life and so does not deceive his wife. Consistent, too, is the policeman who believes regulations must be observed and therefore gives out summonses to jaywalkers and the like.

There exists in the history of culture a rare race of highly talented authors of the extreme Right, whose works provide invaluable material for reflection upon consistency. In France this is the breed of Bossuet, De Maistre, and Maurras. Men of considerable intellectual courage, they have not been afraid to carry their assumptions to their logical conclusions and loudly voice their judgments on every matter in which their principles were engaged.

Joseph de Maistre knows exactly what is the best order of the world, as ordained by God. He knows, too, what is most precious in this order and what is subordinate. Next, he demonstrates his amazing consistency by applying these general assumptions to all concrete questions: The world is so fashioned that evil must exist; given the existence of evil, there must be punishment. This being so, someone must inflict punishment, and that "someone" is an indispensable element in the social order, worthy of respect for that reason. De Maistre then writes in praise of the hangman: "All greatness, all power, the hierarchy as a whole rest upon the hangman: he is the terror and the mainstay of human society. Remove this misconstrued factor from the world and instantly order will yield to chaos, thrones will shake, and society perish. God, who created authority, also created punishment." It follows that the hangman, because his profession is shrouded in dread, "is an anomalous being and to include him in the family of man requires a special dispensation, a fiat of creative power. He was created just as the world was."

Similarly: Spiritual crimes are worse than those of the flesh because the good of the spirit carries more weight. Spiritual crimes are also more odious because they offend against God's majesty, which is greater than that of terrestrial sovereigns; and this leads De Maistre to praise the Spanish Inquisition. In like fashion, Galileo was himself responsible for his trial because he could not refrain from writing despite his promise, because he defended the compatibility between Copernicus and the Bible, because he wrote in the vernacular and not in Latin. De Maistre concludes by lauding the tribunal that found Galileo guilty.

We may salute this fine example of consistency, of strict application of principle. On the other hand, we must note that humanity has survived only thanks to inconsistency.

What is required of a soldier going off to war? Uniquely that he be consistent in his righteous duty to defend his country. (I say "defend" because, as we know, all that seems to exist in wartime is "defense," and always "righteous," at that.) Battles fought by consistent soldiers can end only when the last man on one of the sides gives up the ghost. What is required of a citizen? Consistent loyalty to the state or government. Therefore a consistent citizen will always be proud to cooperate with the secret police, knowing it to be necessary to the existence of the state, to its glory and growth. To prove this is so is the easiest thing in the world, and every citizen who hesitates to write systematically to the secret police informing on his neighbors is surely inconsistent. Let us assume that we consider a certain matter to be the most important in the world; for example, a universal obligation to wear a top hat. Why, then, should we object to imposing our idea by means of war, aggression, provocation, blackmail, assassination, intimidation, terror, murder, or torture?

The race of those who vacillate and are soft, the inconsistent people, precisely those who happily eat steak for dinner but are totally incapable of slaughtering a chicken; those who do not wish to contravene the laws of the land yet do not denounce others to the secret police; those who go to war but in a hopeless situation surrender as prisoners rather than die in a last-ditch fight; those who prize frankness but cannot bring themselves to tell a famous painter that his work is terrible, nervously uttering words of praise which they do not mean—in short, the race of inconsistent people—continues to be one of the greatest sources of hope that possibly the human species will somehow manage to survive. For this is the race of which part believes in God and the superiority of eternal salvation over temporal well-being, yet does not demand that heretics be converted at the stake; while the other part, not believing in God, espouses revolutionary changes in social conditions yet rejects methods purporting to bring about these changes which openly contradict a certain moral tradition in which these people were raised.

In other words, total consistency is tantamount in practice to fanaticism, while inconsistency is the source of tolerance. Why should anyone inflexibly convinced of the exclusive truth of his concepts regarding any and all questions be willing to tolerate opposing ideas? What good can he expect of a situation in which everyone is free to express opinions that to his mind are patently false and therefore harmful to society? By what right should he abstain from using any means whatsoever to attain the goal he regards as correct?

We could say at this point that tolerance is extorted, that the only things tolerated are those which, for lack of ammunition, cannot be destroyed. And as a rule the only people are those who are so strong that their opponents cannot eliminate them with impunity. This observation is certainly well documented by history, but it does not explain everything. If a power relationship were the sole basis of tolerance, and if in addition fanatical consistency ruled the minds of the antagonists, the two groups would be permanently involved in trying to eradicate each other. Since this does not occur, or at least not always, it is only as the blessed result of inconsistency, an inconsistency which does not necessarily spring from conscious acceptance of the principle of tolerance, but merely manifests itself as if that principle were accepted to some degree.

Inconsistency is simply a secret awareness of the contradictions of this world. By contradictions I mean the various values that are, notoriously throughout history, introduced into society by mutually antagonistic forces. If convictions of the absolute and exclusive superiority of a given value to which all else is subordinate were to spread and be practiced widely, they would of necessity transform the world into an ever-larger battleground—which indeed does occur from time to time. The lack of consistency checks this tendency.

Inconsistency as an individual attitude is merely a consciously sustained reserve of uncertainty, a permanent feeling of possible personal error, or if not that, then of the possibility that one's antagonist is right. We have been speaking all this time about the relationship between thinking and the bases of practical action. Now, all thought that can in any way manifest itself as a causative factor in practical conduct is the affirmation of a value. In turn—and this is one of the most important principles we wish to formulate—*the world of values is not logically dualistic*, as opposed to the world of theoretical thought. In other words, there are values that exclude each other without ceasing to be values (although there are no mutually exclusive truths that still remain truths). Daily life shows at every step what a truism this statement is.

Inconsistency, in the sense we use it here, is simply a *refusal once and for all to choose beforehand between any values whatever which mutually exclude each other*. A clear awareness of the eternal and incurable antinomy in the world of values is nothing but conscious inconsistency, though inconsistency is more often practiced than proclaimed. Inconsistency is a constant effort to cheat life, which incessantly tries to place us before alternative doors, each of which is an entrance but through neither of which we can return. Once we have entered we are compelled to fight to the end, to the last bullet, for life or death, with him who entered through the other door. Thus we try to dodge, to maneuver, to use all the tricks and traps, all the suspect manipulations and stratagems, subterfuges and evasions, the chicanery, half-truths, hints, and circumspection—anything to keep from being pushed through either of the doors that opens upon a single direction.

These attempts to deceive life, to conciliate implacable antagonists—these efforts to evade the fatal "either-or" between contradictory values—all this is not the result of a temporary derangement in people's lives that will be removed with the advent of the new era. It is the result of human nature, whose antinomies are always with us. Accepting them as part of man's universal lot, we can elude these antinomies through inconsistency, in order not to reject permanently something we value just because something else we esteem is eternally contradictory to it. So we try to postpone final decisions until the end of life overtakes us, the sole situation in which there is no longer any possibility of choice.

At this point someone may ask: Is this any different from the common-sense wisdom Aristotle set forth in his Nicomachean Ethic? Indeed, his idea is based on the premise that there exist virtues and antivirtues, as well as corresponding vices and antivices. Thrift is a virtue and parsimony a vice; but generosity is also a virtue, while extravagance is wrong. We can—so taught the father of Europe's intellectual tradition—reconcile contradictory virtues without falling prey to the opposite vices. Let us be at once frugal and open-handed, but neither miserly nor prodigal. Let us hold that middle ground between recklessness and cowardice which harmoniously combines valor and prudence. As between a feverish lust for fame and timorous humility, let us seek to maintain a position which unites healthy ambition with modesty. Equally removed from brutal vengefulness and abject submissiveness, let us be both firm and gentle. For the truly generous man is not wasteful but thrifty; just as the courageous man is not reckless but cautious. And so forth.

Have we, in praising inconsistency, come to the point of merely repeating the age-old dictum of the golden mean? Let me confess at once that my idea does not pretend to the slightest consanguinity with this middle-of-the-road theory; it is, in fact, the exact opposite. Aristotle's ethic! Aristotle's ethic was clearly earthly, but his earth was flat. He expounded a novel concept that unified the Hellenistic world. He conquered the world because he was the embodiment of the spirit of universal conciliation at a time when unity was needed most. In metaphysics, politics, and moral doctrine he personified this unity. But Aristotle's genius is alien to us because we live in a world of extremes.

If we look more closely at this Aristotelian ethic we see that its main current is a longing for synthesis and a belief that between any two extremes one can find a mean that will preserve the best of each and reject what is harmful. It is assumed that a reasonable mind can harmonize what to the immoderate one appear to be contradictions. In other words, Aristotle believes that the contradictions in human attitudes that erupt into social antagonisms are not inherent in the world but are caused by lack of reasonableness. Thus antinomies are created by man, who in one way or another misuses the good in the world.

My praise of inconsistency, however, springs from a completely different source. It posits that contradictions in values do not stem from their abuse and therefore are not merely appearances that can be overcome by intelligent moderation. These contradictions inhere in the world of values and cannot be reconciled in any synthesis. Reasonable inconsistency does not seek to forge a synthesis between extremes, knowing it does not exist, since values as such exclude each other integrally. The real world of values is inconsistent; that is to say, it is made up of antagonistic elements. To grant them full recognition simultaneously is impossible, yet each demands total acceptance. This is not a matter of logical contradictions, because values are not theoretical theses. It is a contradiction which lies at the heart of human behavior.

Inconsistency is thus a certain attitude which, having realized that this is the situation, knows the extremes to be irreconcilable yet refuses to reject either because it recognizes each as valid.

Naturally, I do not mean that no concrete conflict of two values clashing in a given situation can ever be reconciled. My thesis is not concerned with any pair of contradictions within a defined context, but with the condition of contradiction as such. In other words, I believe it is possible to synthesize or surmount actual contradictions, but at the same time I am convinced—in accordance with the experience of history as a whole—that one contradiction disappears only to give way to another; that therefore, no universal synthesis is possible. In the world we live in, contradictions cannot be reconciled; once resolved, they pertain no longer to this world but to a dead one, regarding which we need no longer take a practical stand. Contradictions pursue us as long as we act in a world of values, which simply means for as long as we live.

Let us take an example from everyday political life. We believe that nations have the right to decide their own fate. This belief affirms a certain value. We also believe that certain important social institutions preserved in the life of our nation are detrimental to its development. Yet we see unmistakably that our people prize these very institutions highly and obviously have no intention of listening to our arguments on the subject. For instance, we are not only immune to the benefits of religious consolation but deeply convinced, besides, that the continuing influence of religious institutions upon public life is damaging. Nonetheless, this influence not only manifests itself, but undoubtedly does so in accordance with the will of the people. How should we behave? We do not want to renounce either of the opposing principles involved. We do not want to destroy by force and against the people's will an institution manifestly supported by the majority. Nor do we wish to abandon the fight to abolish this institution.

Some might call this a trite situation, one that in no way excludes a synthesis. That synthesis will come about in the course of history. We expect that as people grow sufficiently enlightened the present conflict will cease to exist. Meanwhile, though, we must—with total consistency—strive to educate people so that in the future they will be disposed to accept our concepts and choose of their own free will to extirpate institutions that, in our opinion, hamper the nation's growth.

Unfortunately, this sage advice does not dispel our doubts. Certainly nothing prevents us from believing that in the course of history, measured by the yardstick of generations, the will of the people will undergo such a change, and that their level of maturity will rise to the point where this particular conflict will disappear. Nevertheless, this hope is of fleeting value in practical daily behavior. Let us suppose that in this country I have to vote on whether the teaching of religion should be introduced in public schools, when heretofore there was none; or, on the contrary, whether to discontinue existing religious education. Then I have no other choice: I vote either in agreement with the will of the people, or else in accordance with what I consider their good. I must vote—this obligation has been forced upon me by circumstances beyond my control. I cannot remain consistent toward both my principles at once, but I do not want to forsake either. This example is neither contrived nor exceptional. How many deputies in any number of parliaments vote one way while secretly hoping the opposition will win?

The problem of the antinomy inherent in the principle of tolerance is eternal and eternally unresolved: how to preach and practice tolerance toward ideas and movements which are intolerant. We act against our basic tenet if we silence these ideas and movements by force; we also act against our principle if we tolerate them, for we thus enable them to triumph and destroy the principle of tolerance in social practice. And it is cold comfort under the circumstances to hope that this contradiction will be solved in the process of historical development, either because, having slaughtered all the enemies of tolerance, we shall be able to apply it boundlessly; or else because these movements will in the course of time discard their intolerance. In practical everyday actions and in our daily participation in society, such perspectives help us minimally in making decisions.

These examples are not fictitious. Our lives are bound up in conflicting loyalties that we must choose between in concrete situations. We must break one bond in favor of another, while still not questioning the first. Loyalty to the individual, to one's own outlook on the world, to human communities in which we find ourselves either accidentally or of free choice, loyalty to nations, parties, governments, friends, to ourselves and those close to us, to our own nature and our convictions, to the present and the future, to concrete things and universalities—there are as many insurmountable contradictions as there are loyalties. An authentic synthesis resolving chronic conflicts rarely occurs; most often the supposed synthesis is superficial and fraudulent. We deceive ourselves with it in order to appear consistent, for one of the values instilled in us since childhood is consistency. Our proposition, aimed at making us realize that in these conditions consistency is an ideological fiction, is thus also intended to remove at least one kind of conflict: that which results from a belief in consistency as a value. So, proclaiming the contradictory nature of the world, we strive to attentuate it at least at one point, for, as we see, conflicts multiply because they are misunderstood. In other words, praise of inconsistency is at the same time the rejection of a specific value, that of the consistent life. The contradiction between the value of a consistent life and that of a basically reasonable one belongs to the species of conflict which may perhaps be removed unilaterally—not by synthesis, but by the repudiation of one of the sides to the dispute.

And immediately the question arises: Can we really proclaim the principle of inconsistency in a perfect formulation, which means, in essence, consistently? Is there no sphere of human events for which we can postulate total consistency, thus falling in turn into conflict with the above-mentioned repudiation? We must answer this question affirmatively. Such a sphere does exist. We call such events elementary situations.

Elementary situations are those in which tactics perish; that is, those human situations in which our moral attitude is unchanged regardless of the way these situations arrive at their culmination. If a man is dying of hunger and I can feed him, then there is no confluence of circumstances in which it would be right to say "It is, nevertheless, tactically better to let him die"; or, if I cannot help him, to say "Tactically it is better to hush up the fact that he died of hunger." Open aggression, genocide, torture, mistreatment of the defenseless—all these are elementary situations. In such situations the values of inconsistency cease to play a role, and here we suddenly confront a dual-valued world. In this way our praise of inconsistency is also inconsistent. Inconsistency has certain limits within which it is valid: the limits wherein reality is contradictory. But reality is contradictory only up to a certain point. (We are speaking at all times about the reality of values and not about the reality which is the subject of theoretical speculation.) For let us also carefully bear in mind that to be consistent in inconsistency means to contradict by an act (the application of a certain consistency) something the affirmation of which (the affirmation of inconsistency) is the substance of that act; in short, to fall into an impossible situation, into an antinomy.

Let us therefore also be inconsistent in our inconsistency, and apply the principle of inconsistency to itself. But, someone may reproach us, only then do we practice strict inconsistency, only then do we attain total consistency in the practice of inconsistency—for if we were always inconsistent, but our very inconsistency were completely consistent, then by that very fact we would not always be inconsistent. When, however, we limit our inconsistency, that is, when we are not always inconsistent, only then do we become absolutely inconsistent. In other words, we have arrived at the most classical antinomy of terms: consistent inconsistency is not consistent inconsistency (for it excludes inconsistency itself from the principle of inconsistency); inconsistent inconsistency, on the other hand, is actually consistent inconsistency. To this extent, therefore, we propose to preserve the principle of consistency as a value, by practicing the principle of inconsistency inconsistently. To this extent we mold our praise of inconsistency to a perfect form, protesting against the practice of inconsistency in its perfect form.

So much for praise of inconsistency. The rest cannot be verbalized. The rest must be done.